CITYSPOTS
VENICE

Anwer Bati

Thomas Cook

D1465334

Written by Anwer Bati
Updated by Jo-Ann Titmarsh

Published by Thomas Cook Publishing
A division of Thomas Cook Tour Operations Limited
Company registration No: 1450464 England
The Thomas Cook Business Park, 9 Coningsby Road
Peterborough PE3 8SB, United Kingdom
Email: books@thomascook.com, Tel: +44 (0)1733 416477
www.thomascookpublishing.com

Produced by The Content Works Ltd
Aston Court, Kingsmead Business Park, Frederick Place
High Wycombe, Bucks HP11 1LA
www.thecontentworks.com

Series design based on an original concept by Studio 183 Limited

ISBN: 978-1-84157-920-7

Series Editor: Kelly Anne Pipes
Production/DTP: Steven Collins

Printed and bound in Spain by GraphyCems

Cover photography (Across the canal to Santa Maria) © Ripani Massimo/The Travel
Library Limited/photolibrary.com

CONTENTS

SYMBOLS KEY

The following symbols are used throughout this book:

ⓐ address ☎ telephone 🖷 fax 🆆 website address ⓔ email
🕓 opening times ⊛ public transport connections ❶ important

The following symbols are used on the maps:

𝐢 information office		▨ points of interest
✈ airport		O city
✚ hospital		O large town
▣ police station		○ small town
▤ bus station		═ motorway
▤ railway station		▬ main road
Ⓥ vaporetto		— minor road
✝ cathedral		▬ railway
❶ numbers denote featured cafés & restaurants			

Hotels and restaurants are graded by approximate price as follows:
£ budget price ££ mid-range price £££ expensive

▶ *Take a gondola ride through Venice*

Introduction

The Italian city of Venezia, or Venice, right at the tip of the Adriatic Sea, has always been a source of inspiration for artists, writers and romantics. Its spectacular watery landscape may be familiar the world over, but close up its beauty still has the power to beguile you. And despite its diminutive size, there is so much to see – something alluring or intriguing around virtually every corner.

Perhaps the city is all the more romantic for its fragility. *La Serenissima*, or 'the most serene', as it was once known, is built on a series of small, swampy islands connected by around 400 foot bridges. With the islands gradually sinking on their unstable foundations, rising sea levels threaten to flood the area and destroy some of the world's most precious works of art and architecture. Now is an historic time to visit this historic city.

But tourism is not a new phenomenon in Venice. Touring aristocrats and wealthy visitors have always flocked here to enjoy the city's one-time great wealth, influence and cultural activity. As a naval power and a major port and trading hub in the 13th–15th centuries, affluent local traders and well-heeled philanthropists vied with each other to commission bigger, grander, more ornate buildings and works of art, and culture lovers scrambled to see the results. Fashionable gentlemen and ladies came for the riotous carnival celebrations, banned by successive governments but still alive today.

Now it is mostly tourism that keeps the city alive, protects the historic monuments and stimulates the economy. Travelling around Venice by boat, admiring some of the world's most magnificent art and architecture and taking part in centuries-old festivals and traditions are unique experiences. Prices can be fairly high and the weather can be dull at times, but visitors keep flocking. If you visit too, you will understand why.

◆ *A rainbow over Riva degli Schiavoni*

When to go

Venice welcomes tourists at any time of the year but is particularly busy between Easter and October. This long high season corresponds with high prices, packed accommodation and long queues. The city also fills up over Christmas and New Year and during its carnival in February. The best time to visit is early spring or late autumn to avoid the crowds and high prices, or in November or January if you want a quiet stay and don't mind the cold, damp weather.

SEASONS & CLIMATE

Venice tends to be hot and humid in summer, with the odd thunderstorm. Spring and autumn are mild but wet and the easterly wind can make for chilly evenings. Venice is cold, foggy and damp in winter, which can be romantic if you are well protected and wrapped up warm. High tides and winds (*acqua alta*) in winter can sometimes lead to flooding in the city.

ANNUAL EVENTS

The most important cultural events in Venice, apart from Carnival, are the alternate Art and Architecture Biennale festivals held throughout the summer and the International Film Festival in September. Some of the most attractive celebrations to attend, however, are the smaller, more traditional events such as the gondola race on the feast day of St Mark or the 1,000-year-old ceremony of La Sensa.

January

Regata delle Befana The first of many rowing regattas during the year, held on Epiphany (6 Jan). The race takes place along the

Grand Canal, with usually one or two male competitors per boat dressed as the good witch Befana. According to local legend, Befana visits the city the night before Epiphany and delivers sweets and gifts to good children.

February
Carnevale (Carnival, see page 12) A colourful riot of processions, parties and street theatre in the ten days leading up to Lent.

April
Festa di San Marco The feast day of Venice's patron saint St Mark, 25 April, is celebrated by a gondola race from the island of Sant'Elena to the Punta Della Dogana on the Grand Canal.

May–July
La Sensa 1,000-year-old ceremony off the Lido, in which the mayor of Venice throws a gold ring into the sea to symbolise Venice's 'marriage' to the waters. The event takes place on the Sunday after Ascension Day.

Vogalonga Hundreds of boats take part in a race open to anyone in a rowing vessel, including visitors. The race, held on a Sunday in May or early June, starts at 08.30 from St Mark's Square and is heralded by a cannon shot. ☎ 041 521 0544 Ⓦ www.vogalonga.it

Biennale d'Arte Contemporanea Venice's Biennial Contemporary Arts Festival, founded in 1895, takes place on odd-numbered years and sees both official and unofficial exhibitions and events at various locations including the Giardini park and the Arsenale. ☎ 041 521 8711 Ⓦ www.labiennale.org Ⓛ 10.00–18.00 Tues–Sun, mid June–end Oct. Next arts festival 2009, 2011. Admission charge to official exhibitions.

Biennale d'Architettura (Biennial Architecture Festival) takes place on even-numbered years. Details as for the Biennale d'Arte. Next architecture festival 2008, 2010.

Venezia Suona One-day rock, folk and jazz festival, usually held on a Sunday in late June. ☎ 041 275 0049 🆆 www.veneziasuona.it

Festa del Redentore One of Venice's oldest and most important festivals celebrating the end of the plague of 1576. A pontoon bridge is constructed across the Giudecca canal to the church of Il Redentore on the third weekend in July. Boats and picnickers gather to celebrate and there is a spectacular firework display in the evening.

August–September

Mostra Internazionale D'Arte Cinematografica (Venice International Film Festival, see page 122) One of the world's most important film festivals, based on the Lido.

Circuito Off Venice International Short Film Festival Quieter film festival held over one week in early September on the tiny island of San Servolo. Many films are in English. 🅰 Giudecca 212 ☎ 041 244 6979 🆃 041 244 6930 🆆 www.circuitooff.com

Regata Storica Colourful parade of decorated boats on the first Sunday in September, followed by rowing races with participants wearing historical costumes.

October

Venice Marathon Held between Stra, east of Padua, and the Riva dei Sette Martiri on the last Sunday in October. ☎ 041 532 1871 🆆 www.venicemarathon.it

November

Festa della Salute Festival celebrating the end of the plague of 1630. A bridge of boats is laid across the Grand Canal to the church of Santa Maria della Salute on the 21 November, a public holiday in Venice.

PUBLIC HOLIDAYS

Capodanno (New Year's Day) 1 Jan
La Befana (Epiphany) 6 Jan
Pasqua & Pasquetta (Easter Sunday & Monday) 23–4 Mar 2008, 12–13 Apr 2009
Festa della Liberazione/Festa di San Marco (Liberation Day) 25 Apr
Festa del Lavoro (Labour Day) 1 May
Festa della Repubblica (Anniversary of the Republic) 2 June
Festa di San Giovanni (Feast of Saint John the Baptist) 24 June
Ferragosto (Feast of the Assumption) 15 Aug
Ognissanti (All Saints' Day) 1 Nov
Festa dell'Immacolata (Feast of the Immaculate Conception) 8 Dec
Festa della Salute (Venice only) 21 Nov
Natale (Christmas) 25 Dec
Santo Stefano (Boxing Day) 26 Dec

Businesses, banks and post offices are closed on public holidays and there is limited public transport on 1 May, Christmas Day and New Year's Day. Shops and restaurants tend to stay open on public holidays in Venice, unlike in the rest of Italy.

Carnival

Venice's *carnevale* (carnival), first held in 1162, was the precursor of modern carnivals around the world. Although the name literally means 'farewell to meat' as it was held in the days running up to Lent, the event also signalled a farewell to ordinary social hierarchy and discipline. Masks disguised people's identity and class, leading to a slackening of social mores. Numerous laws were introduced to restrict the festivities, including an outright ban by Napoleon in 1797. Revived but soon banned again in the 1930s by a fascist government, official carnival celebrations only restarted in 1979.

The carnival opens each year on the Sunday ten days before *martedi grasso* (Shrove Tuesday) with a grand procession and the Flight of the Dove – a spectacular event in which a trapeze-walking acrobat or an artificial dove flies from the Campanile to the Doge's Palace. Events centre around St Mark's Square with activities such as face-painting, ice-skating, street theatre and live music throughout the ten days. There are several exclusive parties including the legendary Ridotto ball at the **Monaco Hotel** (W www.monaco.hotelinvenice.com). Details of planned events throughout the carnival, which is run and partly sponsored by the city council, appear on the internet around the end of January. Check W www.carnivalofvenice.com or W www.turismovenezia.it for details.

One major feature of carnival is the fantastic range of elaborate masks available to buy, hire or simply admire – anything from *commedia dell'arte* characters to Disney (see page 24).

Hiring carnival costumes can cost anything from €80 to €600. Try **Nicolao Atelier** (a Cannaregio 2590, Fondamenta della Misericordia t 041 520 7051 W www.nicolao.com) or **Atelier Pietro Longhi** (a San Polo 2604B, Rio Terà Frari t 041 714 478 W www.pietrolonghi.com).

Carnival masks make beautiful but pricey souvenirs

● Spectacular costumes compete for attention during Carnival

CASANOVA

Giovanni Giacomo Casanova (1725–1798) demonstrates perfectly the loose spirit of carnival in 18th-century Venice with his well-known life of drinking, partying and whirlwind affairs.

The tall, dark Italian dandy originally studied clerical law in Venice but his short career in the church was tainted by scandals and he quickly left to join the army. Unsuited to the austere military life, Casanova returned to the attractions of Venice where he saved the life of a rich nobleman – thus ensuring his own wealth and position in society. A practical joke involving a freshly buried corpse went wrong when the victim died of shock, and this combined with a rape allegation drove Casanova to leave the city.

Returning to his home town at the age of 30, he was soon arrested and imprisoned in the Doge's Palace (see page 65) for his interest in witchcraft. The only prisoner ever to escape from here, he travelled all round Europe leaving a trail of extraordinary scandals in his wake and eventually came back to Venice – only to be expelled once again for a vicious satire poking fun at the nobility. Perhaps the most extraordinary fact about this notoriously wild philanderer's life is that he died quietly as a librarian in the Czech Republic.

● If you want to take part in the carnival, book well in advance and be prepared to pay high prices. The opening Sunday, Shrove Tuesday and the weekend are the most lively times but the city can be extremely crowded. Streets become bottle-necked and there is a real danger of small children getting lost or crushed in the crowds.

History

Venice was founded in the middle of the 5th century when the Lombards and other Germanic tribes invaded northern Italy. Fleeing Italians sought refuge on the islands of the Venetian lagoon and in 697 formed a republic ruled by an elected *doge,* or 'duke'. Technically still under Byzantine rule, the community gradually increased its independence and a grand *palazzo* was erected on the site of the present Doge's Palace (see page 65) in the early 9th century.

St Mark was allegedly adopted as the city's patron saint in 828 and the saint's symbol, a winged lion, became the city's emblem. St Mark's Basilica, one of the most popular and impressive buildings in Venice, was originally built as a shrine to his remains in the 9th century.

The Republic of Venice developed a superficially democratic system of government, with elected *doges* staying in power for life but constrained by councils. In reality, the city state was controlled by an oligarchy of nobles and merchants.

It wasn't long before the hardy republic became a military and trading force to be reckoned with. Strong links with the Byzantine empire and a powerful navy allowed the city to defeat several rivals in the area, including Cyprus and Crete, and to take control of large portions of the mainland. Power brought arrogance and aggression abroad. Venetians were foremost in the sacking of Constantinople in 1204, returning to their city with huge amounts of booty.

The 15th century saw the city's zenith, when it was the acknowledged leading power in the eastern Mediterranean and the most substantial naval force in Christendom.

The 16th century brought economic and cultural prosperity but a decline in its military and naval empire. In 1797 Napoleon invaded and deposed the last doge, Ludovico Manin, giving control of the city to the Hapsburg monarchy of Austria. Apart from a short period of French rule (1805–1815), Venice remained part of Austria until joining Italy in 1866.

Although the port and industrial areas at Marghera and the office buildings at Mestre were developed in the early 20th century, with vastly improved rail and road links, Venice's main industry is now tourism.

SINKING CITY

Venice rests precariously on the unstable, swampy islands of a lagoon. It has been gradually sinking for years, but rising sea levels have recently multiplied the threat that the city will be inundated, possibly obliterated, by water.

Already when storm winds blow across the Adriatic sea from the south, the waters pile up and *acqua alta* or 'high water' regularly floods the city. Wooden walkways are erected to help pedestrians get about but the salt water is damaging both the ancient buildings and their foundations. You can often see a line of green algae on the outside of buildings marking the frighteningly high water level.

In 2001 the Italian government set in motion an elaborate dam project in the form of 79 enormous hinged gates to close off the lagoon at high water. The plan is controversial, with many experts believing that frequent gate closings will turn the lagoon into an unhealthy pool of industrial waste and sewage. Venice was declared a World Heritage Site by UNESCO in 1987 but even this status may not be enough to save it from a watery end.

Lifestyle

Compared to the estimated 13 or 14 million tourists who visit the city each year, Venice's native population of just 65,000 is very much outnumbered. High prices and very little industry drives residents either into the hospitality business or into leaving Venice to seek work elsewhere. Very few Venetians now live in the centre.

It is fascinating to see the extent to which Venice's water-borne transport system affects the daily life of locals. With no cars to fill up on a weekly supermarket run, inhabitants tend to shop daily in local grocery stores and bakeries. Postmen, rubbish collectors, doctors and ambulances must all travel by water rather than by road. Even crossing the main 'street', the Grand Canal, can involve a short ride over the water on a *traghetto*.

GONDOLA TRIP

To re-enact a classic image of Venice, take a gondola trip around the canals. The boats take up to six people and singers can be arranged.

The best place to arrange a tour is at an official gondola stop, located at the Valaresso, San Tomà and Ca d'Oro water bus stops; at the railway station and bus terminal; at Fondamenta Bacino Orseolo behind St Mark's Square; on Riva degli Schiavoni; in Campo San Moisè; and on the San Polo side of Rialto Bridge. Prices are fixed officially by the Gondola Board at €80 for 40 mins between 8am–7pm, €100 for 50 mins between 7pm–8am plus €50 for each additional 30 mins. There is no need to pay over the official rate. Most speak some English.

🔺 *Venice's covered market on the Rialto – a taste of local life*

The tourist industry is also a great influence on Venetian lifestyle. The demand for handmade arts and crafts means that many locals have acquired considerable artistic skill, reviving traditional techniques of mask-making, glass-blowing and lace-making. Many speak English. In contrast to other European countries, summer is the time when most Venetians work hardest, taking their holidays only when low tourist season arrives.

Inevitably for such a small and popular place, prices are high all year round and rocket in summer and over Christmas, New Year and during carnival. Cut down on costs by doing as the locals do: use water buses not taxis; choose restaurants away from the centre; and drink your coffee standing at the bar rather than sitting at a table.

Culture

Travelling around the canals by water bus or taxi is the best way to get a flavour of Venice's impressive cultural history. Look out for the different architectural styles. Thirteenth-century Byzantine-influenced palazzos have characteristic simple rounded arches, contrasting with the elaborate pointed arches and tracery of Gothic 14th- and 15th-century buildings such as the Ca' d'Oro (see page 110) and the Doge's Palace (see page 65). Sandstone Renaissance structures with classical columns stand amongst the heavily ornamented baroque buildings of the 17th century, such as Ca' Pesaro (see page 97). There is little modern architecture in Venice and most building work these days is for maintenance and renovation.

Venice's biggest boast in architecture is the hugely influential Andrea di Pietro della Gondola (1508–1580). Nicknamed Palladio after the Greek goddess of wisdom Pallas Athene, his harmonious designs adhere strongly to classical Roman principles and the 'Palladian style' has become a recognised architectural style in itself. Many of his celebrated buildings and churches, scattered around Venice and the Veneto region, were given special status in 1994 as a UNESCO World Heritage Site known as the *Palladian Villas of the Veneto*.

Venice's many churches, each set in their own small square, or *campo*, are not only architecturally delightful in themselves but also boast works of art which would grace any major museum.

Venetian artists over the years have left a hoard of valuable paintings reflecting the wealth of their city and the sophistication and finery of some of its citizens. Paolo Veneziano and his contemporaries in the 14th century, influenced by Byzantine art, were the first painters to make a lasting mark on the art world but it was the brothers Giovanni and Gentile Bellini, in the following century, who became internationally famous for their vivid, colourful style. Many of their works can be found in the Correr Museum (see page 70).

The greatest Venetian masters from the 16th century onwards, including Titian, Veronese, Giorgione and Tintoretto, began to use oil rather than egg-based tempera paint. This allowed them to exploit more fully the subtle use of light, shade, atmosphere and texture. You can see some of their finest and best-known works in the Accademia gallery (see page 84).

The 18th century saw the last great movement of Venetian art with painters such as Giambattista Tiepolo, and his son Giandomenico. Canaletto is probably the most famous 18th-century landscape painter ever. Many of his classic images of Venice are now in Britain, bought by aristocrats on the Grand Tour.

If you are interested in modern art try to visit during the Biennale, a major contemporary arts festival held every two years in summer and packed with fantastic exhibitions (see page 9). There are also

🔺 *La Fenice opera house hosts opera, drama and ballet*

some excellent collections of modern art at the Guggenheim Museum (see page 86), Palazzo Grassi (see page 66) and Ca' Pesaro.

If you enjoy the performing arts and you speak Italian it is worth seeing a play at the beautiful **Teatro Carlo Goldoni** (🅐 San Marco 4650B, Calle Goldoni 🟠 041 240 201 🟠 www.teatrostabileveneto.it 🟠 Water bus to Rialto). There are also performances of opera, dance and ballet at the La Fenice opera house (see feature, page 64) and the Teatro Malibran (see page 118). Contemporary dance events are usually held at the Teatro Fondamente Nuove (see page 118).

Concerts of classical music and opera are held around the city and are particularly pleasant when held in a church. There is the occasional live jazz session but strict noise-reduction laws mean concerts of rock and other contemporary music are rare. Book well in advance for major concerts, particularly during peak season.

COMBINED TICKETS

If you are planning to visit several cultural attractions in the city it is well worth getting a combined ticket. You can browse the various options at any tourist office and at the ACTV-Vela offices at Piazzale Roma and near St Mark's Square (🟠 041 2424 🟠 08.00–20.00).

The **Chorus Pass** allows you entrance to Venice's main churches and is available from any of the churches which charge for entry.

The **Venice Card**, which entitles you to free public transport, use of public toilets and entry to various sights and attractions, is another good option. See 🟠 www.venicecard.com.

🟠 *The canals offer intimate glimpses of Venice*

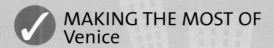

Shopping

Venice's designer clothes shops are clustered around the Mercerie area near St Mark's Square, including some excellent leather shoe and accessory shops.

Skilled artisans selling their arts and crafts are mostly based around Campo Santo Stefano, Calle della Mandola, and the Dorsoduro district. The art of making marbled paper was revived in the 70s and you will see several styles of beautiful paper and other stationery on offer.

There are some good antiques shops clustered around Campo San Maurizio, near St Mark's Square. Look out for rich local fabrics, jewellery, metalwork and old prints.

LOCAL SPECIALITIES

Genuine local specialities from Venice can make fine gifts or souvenirs. Look out for some beautiful lace, marbled paper, glass and carnival masks, produced by skilled local artisans. Glass is best bought on the island of Murano (see page 135), where you can see the glass objects being blown, and lace is particularly fine on Burano (see page 137). However, be wary of shops selling inferior, imported versions of these products. Be prepared to pay for quality.

The traditional art of mask-making was revived in Venice in 1979 and there are several shops making *papier mâché* masks from scratch. Two of the best are **Mondo Novo** (Ⓐ Dorsoduro 3063, Rio Terra Canal ☎ 041 528 7344 ⏰ 09.00–18.30 Mon–Sat ⛴ Water bus to Ca' Rezzonico) and **Papier Mâché** (Ⓐ Castello 5175, Calle Lunga Santa Maria Formosa ☎ 041 522 9995 ⏰ 09.00–19.30 Mon–Sat, 10.00–19.00 Sun ⛴ Water bus to Rialto).

USEFUL SHOPPING PHRASES

What time do the shops open/close?
A che ora aprono/chiudono i negozi?
Ah keh awra ahprawnaw/kewdawnaw ee nehgotsee?

How much is this?
Quant'è?
Kwahnteh?

Can I try this on?
Posso provarlo?
Pawssaw prawvarrlaw?

My size is ...
La mia taglia è ...
Lah meeyah tahlyah eh ...

I'll take this one, thank you
Prenderò questo, grazie
Prehndehroh kwestaw, grahtsyeh

Can you show me the one in the window/this one?
Può mostrarmi quello in vetrina/questo?
Poohoh mawstrahrmee kwehllaw een vehtreenah/kwehstaw?

This is too large/small/expensive
Questo è troppo grande/piccolo/caro
Kwestaw eh tropaw grahndeh/tropaw peekawlaw/trawpaw kahraw

The most colourful food market is at the Rialto Bridge (🕐 07.30–13.00 Mon–Sat). On the San Polo side of the bridge are stalls selling clothes, leather goods and souvenirs. There is a quieter food market in Via Garibaldi in the Castello district (🕐 08.00–12.30 Mon–Sat 🚤 Water bus to Giardini), and a regular market in Rio Terra di San Leonardo in Cannaregio (🕐 08.00–12.30 Mon–Sat 🚤 Water bus to San Marcuola or Guglie).

Eating & drinking

There is a huge choice of places to eat and drink in Venice, ranging
from ordinary bars and cafés to *bacari* (casual wine bars which serve
tapas-style snacks called *cichetti*), more sophisticated *enoteche*
(wine bars with more elaborate food), simple *trattorias* and *osterias*,
plus the more formal *ristorante*. You will also find *pizzerias*, *gelaterie*
(ice cream parlours), tea shops, bakeries, and some excellent cake
and pastry shops.

This huge choice of eateries, though, makes it all the more
important to pick carefully in order to get a good meal at a reasonable
price. Most restaurants near St Mark's Square cater solely for the
tourist industry and as a general rule, the closer you are to this area
the pricier a meal or a drink will be. Cheaper and better quality food
and wine can often be found in the outlying areas such as Cannaregio
(see page 106), Castello (see page 60), San Polo and Santa Croce
(see page 94).

Upmarket hotel restaurants are usually a good bet and can
often be less expensive than what appears to be a more casual
place. Hotel restaurants also stay open on Sunday and Monday
evenings, when many other establishments are closed.

Picnicking on the mini-pizzas, *panini* (toasted sandwiches),
tramezzini (regular sandwiches) and other snacks you can buy

PRICE CATEGORIES

Based on the average cost of a three-course evening meal
for one person, excluding drinks.

£ up to €30   ££ €30–70   £££ over €70

LOCAL SPECIALITIES & WINE

There are many tasty local specialities in Venice, particularly fish and seafood. Try *anguilla* (eel), *baccalà* (a salt cod dip), *folpi* (baby octopus), *granchio* (crab), *granseola* (spider crab), *sarde in soar* (sardines marinated with onions, pine nuts, raisins and vinegar) or, for a more filling meal, *risotto di mare* or *in nero* (seafood risotto or risotto with squid ink).

If you prefer meat, there is some excellent *carpaccio* (raw, lean, thinly sliced fillet of beef), *prosciutto San Daniele* (local ham), *fegato alla veneziana* (calves' liver and onions) and *tripa* (tripe, usually served with onions). Common pre-dinner snacks are *acciuge* (anchovies) or *boveleti* (small snails). You can nibble on these while enjoying a *spritz*, a favourite Venetian aperitif consisting of white wine, Campari and soda.

Local wine from the Veneto region, the hinterland behind Venice, is good quality and generally better value than imported varieties. Look out for Valpolicella (a full-bodied red sometimes drunk chilled), Bardolino (another robust red which goes well with meat), Soave (a smooth white), Raboso (a warming, tannic red) and Valadige (red, white or rosé). Wines labelled *superiore* or *classico* tend to be reliable. The region's trademark light sparkling wine, Prosecco, is normally drunk as an aperitif.

Grappa is a strong brandy drunk after dinner and the other local liqueur of choice is the sweet, almond-flavoured Amaretto. Ask your waiter for his advice on the several excellent local dessert wines.

in cafés and bakeries is pleasant along the Zattere, by the Giudecca canal (see page 80). Picnicking in most other areas is frowned on, however, and there are few benches or quiet areas in which to sit.

Many restaurants add an often hefty cover charge to the bill on top of the price of the meal – check before sitting down. A service charge is usually included in the price so it is normal simply to round up the bill to the nearest euro. When service is specifically not included, a tip of ten percent is fine.

If you visit in peak season and plan to eat in a particular restaurant, make sure you book in advance. If you visit in low season, be aware that some restaurants and bars may be closed.

● *Enjoying an al fresco meal in Campo del Piovan*

ⓘ Italy now has some of the strictest anti-smoking laws in Europe. Smoking in public buildings or enclosed spaces such as restaurants and bars is strictly forbidden except at outside tables and in designated smoking rooms.

USEFUL DINING PHRASES

I would like a table for ... people
Vorrei un tavolo per ... persone
Vawrray oon tahvawlaw perr ... perrsawneh

Waiter/waitress!
Cameriere/cameriera!
Cahmehryereh/cahmehryera!

May I have the bill, please?
Mi dà il conto, per favore?
Mee dah eel cawntaw, perrfahvawreh?

Could I have it well-cooked/medium/rare please?
Potrei averlo ben cotto/mediamente cotto/poco cotto, per favore?
Pawtray ahvehrlaw behn cawtaw/mehdeeyahmehnteh cawtaw/pawcaw cawtaw perr fahvawreh?

I am a vegetarian. Does this contain meat?
Sono vegetariano/vegetariana. Contiene carne?
Sawnaw vejetahreeahnaw/vejetahreeahnah.
Contyehneh kahrneh?

Entertainment & nightlife

Carnival excepted, Venice's nightlife tends to be relaxed and quiet. Lazy dinners and evening strolls are more popular than loud music and wild dancing, and many bars and cafés close by 22.00 or earlier. Restaurants tend to stop serving at 22.30 or 23.00. For late-night activity, head for Campo Santa Margherita, Campo Santo Stefano, Campo San Polo, Fondamenta della Misericordia and Campo San Barnaba. Some upmarket restaurants have bars that stay open late.

Strict legislation regarding noise levels means that live and open-air music events are not common in the city. Look out for posters advertising classical concerts in churches instead, and you will enjoy an evening of peaceful music in beautiful surroundings.

Venice's International Film Festival in late August and early September (see page 122) draws hordes of film stars and cinema lovers to the Lido and is one time when Venice becomes much more lively than usual. For a quieter cinema event go for the Circuito Off Venice International Short Film Festival (see page 10), held around the same time on the tiny island of San Servolo.

In addition, every evening in summer there are open-air film screenings in Campo San Polo (❶ 041 524 4347 ❷ 21.00 ❶ Most films are in Italian, except during the Venice

● *Evening entertainment at a casino*

ROMANTIC VENICE

Many Venetians take a stroll after dinner and stop off on the way home for coffee or an ice cream. Walking around Venice at night, particularly when it's warm, can be a romantic and pleasant experience. Taking a gondola, water bus or taxi along the Grand Canal is another night-time pleasure.

Film Festival. Admission charge). There are also two regular cinemas in the city. Films at **Giorgione Movie** (🅐 Cannaregio 4612, Rio Terra dei Franceschi 🕾 041 522 6298 🌐 www.comune.venezia.it/cinema 🚢 Water bus to Ca' d'Oro) are mostly dubbed into Italian, though there is a winter programme of films shown in their original language on Tuesdays. If you are on the Lido try the **Multisala Astra** (🅐 Via Corfù 9, Lido 🕾 041 526 5736 🚢 Water bus to Lido).

TICKETS & LISTINGS INFORMATION

For detailed listings of upcoming concerts visit 🌐 www.turismovenezia.it.

A good fortnightly listings publication in Italian and English is *Un Ospite di Venezia*, available free from hotels and tourist offices or on-line at 🌐 www.unospitedivenezia.it. For jazz, check 🌐 www.caligola.it.

Tickets for most events are available from **ACTV-Vela** 🅐 Santa Croce 509, Piazzale Roma 🕘 08.30–18.30 or 🅐 San Marco 1810, Calle dei Fuseri 🕘 08.30–18.30 Mon–Sat. Call 🕾 041 2424 or see 🌐 www.hellovenezia.com for more information.

Sport & relaxation

SPECTATOR SPORTS

Football Venice's football club AC Venezia play at **Stadio PL Penzo** in Sant'Elena (🔵 Viale Sant'Elena 🕐 Games Sat & Sun, June–Sept 🆆 www.veneziacalcio.it 🅽 Water bus to Sant'Elena). For tickets contact **HelloVenezia** (📞 041 2424 🆆 www.hellovenezia.com).

PARTICIPATION SPORTS

Cycling Cycling is popular on the Lido. For bicycle hire try **Lido On Bike** (🔵 Gran Viale 21B 📞 041 526 8019 🆆 www.lidoonbike.it) or **Giorgio Barberi** (🔵 Gran Viale 79A 📞 041 526 1490).

Golf The **Circolo Golf Venezia** on the Lido has beaches and a golf club (🔵 Strada Vecchia 1 📞 041 731 333 🆆 www.circologolfvenezia.it 🅽 Water bus to Lido).

Gym Try the **Palestra International Club** (🔵 Sotoportego dei Amai 📞 041 528 9830 🅽 Water bus to Rialto) or the **Eutonia Club** (🔵 Calle Renier, Dorsoduro 📞 041 522 8618 🆆 www.eutonia.net 🅽 Water bus to Ca' Rezzonico).

Rowing You can try your hand at rowing – and even participate in the local regattas – at one of Venice's rowing clubs. For lessons contact **Reale Societa Canottieri Bucintoro** (🔵 Zattere, Dorsoduro 15 📞 041 522 2055 🆆 www.bucintoro.org).

Swimming For a luxurious hotel swimming pool and spa, visit the **Cipriani** on the island of Giudecca (🔵 Giudecca 10 📞 041 520 7745 🆆 www.hotelcipriani.com 🅽 Water bus to Zitelle). There are also three public pools: **Piscina Comunale Di Sant'Alvise** (ⓐ Calle del Capitello, Campo Sant'Alvise ⓣ 041 715 650 ⓦ Water bus to Sant'Alvise), **Piscina Comunale Sacca Fisola** on the island of Giudecca (ⓐ San Biagio-sacca Fisola, Giudecca ⓣ 041 528 5430 ⓦ Water bus to Sacca Fisola) and **Piscina Ca' Bianca** (ⓐ Via Sandro Gallo, Lido ⓣ 041 526 2222 ⓦ Water bus to Lido. Opening times vary).

Tennis You can play tennis and rent racquets at **Tennis Club Ca' del Moro** on the Lido (ⓐ Via Ferruccio Parri 6 ⓣ 041 770 965 ⓛ 08.30–21.00 Mon–Fri, 08.30–20.00 Sat & Sun ⓦ Water bus to Lido then Bus: V). The club also has a gym and swimming pool.

RELAXATION
Centro Benessere in the Cipriani hotel offers massage, skincare, hot stones, manicures and a hairdresser. Open to non-hotel guests (ⓐ Giudecca 10 ⓣ 041 240 8016 ⓦ www.hotelcipriani.com ⓦ Water bus to Zitelle).

🔺 *Relaxing in a gondola*

Accommodation

Staying in one of Venice's many upmarket hotels or traditional canal-side guest houses can be a great experience but is also expensive. As a general rule, the closer you stay to St Mark's Square or the Grand Canal, the more you will pay. You can often find good deals through tour operators or websites, particularly if you book well in advance, avoid peak season and visit during the week rather than at the weekend.

Some hotels include a continental or buffet breakfast in their rates but others charge a hefty supplement so do check before booking.

For more information see the helpful Venice tourist information website: Ⓦ www.turismovenezia.it

HOTELS

Agli Alboretti £–££ Popular hotel near the Accademia with a good restaurant and pleasant rooms. ❸ Dorsoduro 882, Rio Terra Foscarini ❶ 041 523 0058 Ⓦ www.aglialboretti.com Ⓝ Water bus to Accademia

Hotel Rio £–££ Comfortable, modern hotel run by the owner of the nearby Aciugheta restaurant. Not all rooms have en suite bathrooms. ❸ Castello 4356, Campo Santii Filippo e Giacomo ❶ 041 523 4810 Ⓦ www.aciugheta-hotelrio.it Ⓝ Water bus to San Zaccaria

PRICE CATEGORIES
Based on the average price per night for two people sharing a double room. Some rooms, particularly those overlooking canals, may be more expensive.

£ up to €150   ££ €150–250   £££ over €250

Locanda del Ghetto £–££ A small, modest hotel with pleasant rooms.
🅐 Cannaregio 2892, Campo del Ghetto Nuovo ☏ 041 275 9292
🆆 www.locandadelghetto.net ⦿ Water bus to San Marcuola

Locanda San Barnaba £–££ Centrally located hotel with 13 spacious
rooms. 🅐 Dorsoduro 2785-6, Calle del Traghetto ☏ 041 241 1233
🆆 www.locanda-sanbarnaba.com ⦿ Water bus to Ca' Rezzonico

Al Ponte Mocenigo ££ On the other side of a private bridge,
this good value hotel is tastefully decorated and charming.
🅐 Santa Croce 2063, Fondamenta Rimpeto Mocenigo ☏ 041 524 4797
🆆 www.alpontemocenigo.com ⦿ Water bus to San Stae

Ca' Pisani ££ Art deco style in an old merchant's house near the
Accademia. 🅐 Dorsoduro 979A ☏ 041 240 1411 🆆 www.capisanihotel.it
⦿ Water bus to Accademia

Ca' Vendramin di Santa Fosca ££ Small hotel in an old *palazzo*
near a quiet canal. 🅐 Cannaregio 2400 ☏ 041 275 0125
🆆 www.hotelcavendramin.it ⦿ Water bus to Ca' d'Oro

La Calcina ££ This charming hotel on the Zattere, overlooking
the Redentore and the Giudecca Canal, also has apartments.
🅐 Dorsoduro 780, Fondamenta delle Zattere ☏ 041 520 6466
🆆 www.lacalcina.com ⦿ Water bus to Zattere

Oltre Il Giardino ££ Intimate, tranquil boutique hotel with
a garden. 🅐 San Polo 2542, Fondamenta Contarini ☏ 041 275 0015
🆆 www.oltreilgiardino-venezia.com ⦿ Water bus to San Tomà

Cipriani £££ More a resort than a hotel, located on the island of Giudecca. Swimming pool, spa and other facilities, including three restaurants. ⓐ Giudecca 10 ⓣ 041 520 7745 ⓦ www.hotelcipriani.com ⓝ Water bus to Zitelle; Private launch from St Mark's Square

Danieli £££ One of Venice's most famous hotels in the former home of a *doge*. Impressive décor and roof terrace. ⓐ Castello 4196, Riva degli Schiavoni ⓣ 041 522 6480 ⓦ www.starwoodhotels.com ⓝ Water bus to San Zaccaria

Gritti Palace £££ Reputed hotel by the Grand Canal decorated with priceless antiques. ⓐ Campo Santa Maria del Giglio 2467 ⓣ 041 79 4611 ⓦ www.starwoodhotels.com ⓝ Water bus to San Zaccaria

Hilton Molino Stucky £££ Set in a converted former flour mill, this hotel offers all the comforts of a luxury hotel in the shell of an industrial building. ⓐ Giudecca 753, Fondamenta San Biagio ⓣ 041 272 3311 ⓦ www.hilton.com/venice ⓝ Water bus to Palanca; Private launch from St Mark's Square and the Zattere by arrangement

B&BS

Al Gallion £ Immaculate 16th-century *palazzo* tucked away behind Campo San Giacomo dell'Orio. ⓐ Santa Croce 1126, Calle Gallion ⓣ 041 524 4743 ⓦ www.algallion.com ⓝ Water bus to Riva di Biasio

Ca' Miani £ Owned by French hairdresser Pascal Cariou, this central B&B is stylish and tranquil. ⓐ San Marco 2865, Calle del Frutarol ⓣ 041 241 1868 ⓝ Water bus to San Samuele

◀ *The omni-present Molino Stucky Hilton on the Giudecca*

Ca' Della Corte ££ A finely decorated 16th-century house with a courtyard. Rooms are bright and spacious. ⓐ Dorsoduro 3560, Corte Surian ⓣ 041 71 5877 ⓦ www.cadellacorte.com ⓝ Water bus to Piazzale Roma

Palazzo Malcanton ££ Lavishly restored 15th-century house with a garden. Near the station and Piazzale Roma. ⓐ Santa Croce 49, Salizada San Pantalon ⓣ 041 71 0931 ⓦ www.venice4you.co.uk ⓝ Water bus to Piazzale Roma

HOSTELS

Most hostels have double rooms as well as larger dormitories and charge around €25–€50 per room per night.

Casa Santa Dorotea £ ⓐ Cannaregio 2927 ⓣ 041 71 7022 ⓝ Water bus to Guglie

Residenza Universitaria San Toma £ ⓐ San Polo 2846 ⓣ 041 275 0930 ⓦ www.esuvenezia.it ⓝ Water bus to San Tomà

● *Classic Venetian style at the Danieli Hotel*

THE BEST OF VENICE

Make the most of a short trip to Venice by fitting in as many as possible of its fantastic sights and attractions, but take the time to relax and enjoy the city's special atmosphere as well.

TOP 10 ATTRACTIONS

- **St Mark's Basilica** The oldest and most famous building in Venice is part of the city's soul (see page 60).

- **Boat trips on the canals** Take a water bus from the airport, Lido or islands or splash out on a water taxi or gondola ride. One of the best ways to travel around Venice, see its impressive buildings and churches and re-live its history (see page 55).

- **Piazza San Marco & the Campanile** The heart of the city, with museums and shopping all around. You can get great views of Venice from the top of the Campanile, or bell tower (see pages 62 & 64).

- **Accademia Gallery** The place to see the works of the city's greatest artists (see page 84).

- **Rialto Bridge** One of the focal points of the city with a buzzing market (see page 94).

- **Ca' Rezzonico** If you want to know how Venetians used to live, this is the place to go (see page 83).

- **Murano & Burano** Tiny islands where the traditional skills of glass- and lace-making remain alive (see page 130).

- **Santa Maria Gloriosa dei Frari** Perhaps the most important church in Venice, with works by Titian and Giovanni Bellini (see page 97).

- **Peggy Guggenheim Collection** Venice's finest collection of modern art in a popular but peaceful museum on the Grand Canal (see page 86).

- **Ca' d'Oro** This 15th-century merchant's *palazzo* has an astounding façade and boasts an impressive collection of paintings (see page 110).

▼ *The magnificence of St Mark's Basilica*

Suggested itineraries

HALF-DAY: VENICE IN A HURRY
Head to the heart of the city, St Mark's Square, where you'll find most main sights, attractions and shops. Have a drink in the legendary Florian or Quadri cafés, take the lift to the top of the Campanile, and admire St Mark's Basilica. Then choose between shopping in the nearby arts and crafts shops (see page 24), art in the Correr Museum (see page 70), or history in the Doge's Palace (see page 65). If the weather is good, take a water bus, water taxi or gondola down the Grand Canal to see Venice from another perspective.

1 DAY: TIME TO SEE A LITTLE MORE
A full day in Venice means you can also visit the Accademia gallery (see page 84) and see the greatest glories of Venetian art. Ca' Rezzonico (see page 83) is nearby and will give you an idea of the lush interior design during Venice's heyday. Find time to walk across Rialto Bridge in the morning and soak up the atmosphere of its lively food market (see page 94).

2–3 DAYS: TIME TO SEE MUCH MORE
When you've discovered the city centre and want to escape the day-tourists, head for the Dorsoduro (see page 80), Santa Croce and San Polo areas (see page 94). In Dorsoduro, you will find the famous Peggy Guggenheim Collection (see page 86) and the nearby church of Santa Maria della Salute, one of the city's major landmarks. Santa Croce and San Polo contain the magnificent church of Santa Maria Gloriosa dei Frari (see page 97) and the Scuola Grande di San Rocco (see page 98). Relax at a café or restaurant along Zattere with a view of the island of Giudecca

(see page 80). Treat yourself by popping into Harry's Bar (see page 76) or the Gritti Palace hotel (see page 37) for a drink.

LONGER: ENJOYING VENICE TO THE FULL

To get away from the bustle, head to Cannaregio for the lovely church of Madonna dell'Orto (see page 108). If you are interested in ships and naval history, don't miss the Museo Storico Navale in the Arsenale area (see page 72). You should also make time for a trip to the island of Giudecca (see page 120), where you will have fine views of Venice and can enjoy a drink at the luxurious Cipriani hotel (see page 37). For a change in atmosphere and some time on the beach, go to the Lido (see page 120). Alternatively, head out to the charming small islands of Torcello, Murano and Burano (see page 130).

● *Santa Maria della Salute is a useful, beautiful landmark*

Something for nothing

Venice is not the place to come for a cheap holiday. The cost of accommodation, restaurant prices, and admission fees for museums and attractions are all relatively high, particularly over summer, Christmas and carnival.

On the other hand, some of the most enjoyable things about the city are absolutely free. Strolling down the canals, standing on the bridges, admiring the views, soaking up the atmosphere, chatting and pointing, are a real pleasure when there are no cars to distract you from the stunningly beautiful architecture. Treat the streets as a museum and take closer looks at the impressive buildings and elaborate designs you will come across.

Many arts, crafts and antiques on sale in the shops are worth admiring in their own right, even if you don't plan to buy. For an unforgettably romantic experience on a budget stroll down the Grand Canal at sunset.

People-watching is a favoured pastime, especially in summer when street entertainers and buskers abound. For a lazy afternoon in a free park, try the gardens in the Castello district (see page 60) or the Giardini Pubblici (see page 60).

Churches charge lower admission fees than museums but often contain artworks that are just as impressive. Look out for posters advertising free concerts in churches.

Some of the most lively events in Venice – its colourful rowing regattas and other annual events (see page 8) – are completely free. For rare free rock, reggae and jazz concerts check out the Venezia Suona music festival in June (see page 10).

▶ *The magic of sunset*

When it rains

If it rains in Venice – which it often does – you'll see a different but no less fascinating side of the city. Instead of sitting outside a café in one of the squares, soak up the special atmosphere indoors. Try the Florian café in St Mark's Square (see page 62) with its wood panelling and mirrored interiors, or the lushly decorated Harry's Bar (see page 76).

Rain means you can safely spend longer admiring and appreciating the magnificent works of art in churches and museums. The Basilica of San Marco (see page 60) and the Palazzo Ducale (see page 65) should certainly feature on any rainy day itinerary. Shopping for arts, crafts and designer goods can also be rewarding, and the Rialto market buzzes whatever the weather. A ride in a water bus or water taxi under cover will give you a different perspective on the buildings you see – you will spend less time photographing and more time simply looking.

Venice's nightlife tends to be quiet and based indoors in restaurants, theatres or concert halls, so rain shouldn't make too much difference to your evening entertainment.

It can rain at any time of the year in Venice and there are frequent heavy thunderstorms in summer, so do come prepared with umbrellas, raincoats and strong walking shoes whenever you visit. A look at ⓦ www.weather.com or ⓦ www.bbc.co.uk/weather will let you know what to expect. Thankfully, rain showers do not tend to last long and in summer the streets will dry very quickly.

● *Ca' d'Oro: the best-known palazzo on the Grand Canal*

On arrival

TIME DIFFERENCE
Italian clocks follow Central European Time (CET), one hour ahead of Greenwich Mean Time (GMT). Clocks go forward one hour at the end of March and back one hour at the end of October.

ARRIVING
By air
Venice's main airport is **Marco Polo** (☎ 041 260 9260 ⓦ www.veniceairport.it), around 8 km (5 miles) from the city. It has all the usual facilities, including ATMs, bureaux de change, information and accommodation booking desks, shops and a bar.

ATVO coaches (☎ 0421 594 518 ⓦ www.atvo.it) to the city centre run roughly every 30 minutes until 00.20, with tickets on sale from the ATVO desk near baggage reclaim. Journey time is 20 minutes. Note that the last bus leaving Venice for Marco Polo airport on your return journey is at 20.40.

ACTV city buses (☎ 041 2424 ⓦ www.actv.it) also run from Marco Polo airport to Piazzale Roma roughly every 15–30 minutes between 04.08–01.10. The journey takes around 25 minutes and you must purchase a separate ticket for each large suitcase. Tickets can be bought at the ticket machine by the bus stop or from the driver and must be validated on board.

A taxi to Piazzale Roma takes around 20 minutes and you can pay in advance by credit card in the arrivals lounge. Note that land buses and taxis cannot go everywhere in Venice, so you may have to walk or take a water bus from Piazzale Roma to your accommodation.

You can also reach the city centre by water, which is more exciting but also more expensive. **Alilaguna** (☎ 041 523 5775

 www.alilaguna.com) runs an hourly ferry service from the airport along three routes, with connections to St Mark's Square, San Zaccaria, Arsenale, Zattere, the Lido and the island of Murano. Journey time is roughly one hour. Tickets are on sale in the arrivals lounge or on board the ferry, which leaves from the landing stage, a ten-minute walk from the terminal.

▲ Water buses are a good way to get around

Transfer by water taxi is expensive at around €90 to the city centre. You can book one in the arrivals lounge from **Consorzio Motoscafi Venezia** (☎ 041 541 5084 🌐 www.motoscafivenezia.it) or simply wait on the landing stage, but note that only cash is accepted.

Ryanair and some other airlines land at the tiny airport at **Treviso** (☎ 0422 315 111 🌐 www.trevisoairport.it), around 40 km (25 miles) from Venice. The airport has limited facilities and a coach or taxi to the centre takes at least 45 minutes. **ATVO coaches** are timed to coincide with the arrival of Ryanair flights and will wait if a flight is delayed. Contact ATVO (☎ 0422 315 381 🌐 www.atvo.it) for more information.

By rail

Venice's **Santa Lucia** station, in the Cannaregio area on the Grand Canal opposite Piazzale Roma, has an information desk (🕐 07.00–21.00), tourist office (🕐 08.00–18.30), ATMs and some snack bars. You can get a water bus (no. 1 or 82) or water taxi down the Grand Canal from the stops immediately opposite the station entrance. For information on rail travel within Italy, call ☎ 89 20 21 (from within Italy) or see 🌐 www.trenitalia.it. ❶ Make sure you don't get off at Venezia Mestre station on the mainland unless you are actually staying there.

By road

International coach services and national buses stop at the terminal on Piazzale Roma, from where you can walk to your accommodation or take the water bus or water taxi down the Grand Canal.

Venice is connected to major motorways but it is not a good idea to bring a car to the city. Cars can get no further than Piazzale Roma and parking charges are high. In peak periods it is advisable to reserve

IF YOU GET LOST, TRY ...

Excuse me, do you speak English?
Mi scusi, parla inglese?
Mee scoozee, parrla eenglehzeh?

Is this the right way to the old town/the city centre/the tourist office/the station/the bus station?
È questa la strada per la città vecchia/per il centro città/
per l'ufficio informazioni turistiche/per la stazione ferroviaria/
per la stazione degli autobus?
Eeh kwehstah lah strahda perr lah cheetta vehkyah/
perr il chentraw cheetteh/perr looffeechaw eenforrmahtsyawnee
tooreesteekeh/perr la stahtsyawneh ferrawvyarya/
per la stahtsyawneh delee ahootawboos?

a space in the **ASM car park** (ⓐ Piazzale Roma, Santa Croce 496
ⓣ 041 272 7211 ⓦ www.asmvenezia.it) or the **Venezia Tronchetto Parking**
(ⓐ Isola Nova de Tronchetto 1 ⓣ 041 520 7555 ⓦ www.veniceparking.it).

If you do have a car it is best to take the ferry and stay on the
Lido, where travel and parking are easier. Regular ferries run from
Tronchetto to the San Nicolò ferry terminal on the Lido. Contact
ACTV (ⓣ 041 2424 ⓦ www.actv.it) for more information.

FINDING YOUR FEET
The centre of Venice is entirely pedestrianised so your transport
options are limited to walking or catching a water taxi or bus. You
will soon get used to this, but take care when walking along canals

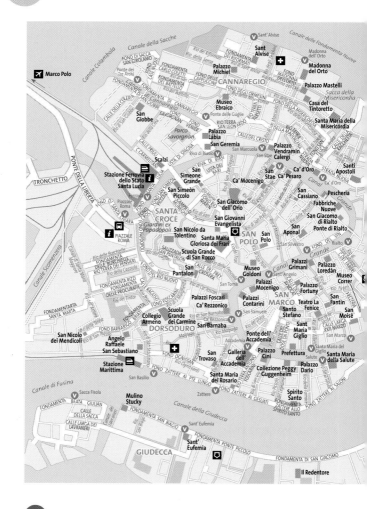

and when boarding waterborne transport. Wear sensible shoes and avoid carrying heavy luggage.

The Venetian dialect is a variant of standard Italian so some street names and signs may be slightly different to those on the map. *Terra*, for example, is often written as *terà*. *Campo* refers to a small square and a *fondamenta* (sometimes *fondamente*) is a road running along a canal.

ORIENTATION

The very things that make Venice attractive – its warren of small canals, its bridges, its passageways – can also make it confusing. It is a good idea to get hold of a detailed map with a street index from the tourist office. There is an excellent interactive map on ⓦ www.veniceonline.it.

Piazza San Marco, or Saint Mark's Square, is the largest square in the city. From here you can easily reach many parts of the city on foot, with major landmarks such as Rialto, to the northwest, and Accademia, to the west, clearly signposted. The Grand Canal, spanned by three bridges, snakes southwest through Venice in an inverted 's' from Piazzale Roma to the huge baroque church of Santa Maria della Salute.

ADDRESSES

Buildings in Venice are numbered according to *sestiere* (district) rather than street. There are six districts: San Marco, Castello, Cannaregio, San Polo, Santa Croce and Dorsoduro. Addresses are usually written with house or building number and district only, eg San Polo 1234, which can make it difficult to find your destination. The street name is given wherever possible in this guide.

GETTING AROUND

Vaporetti (water buses) are run by ACTV (🅐 Offices at Santa Croce, Piazzale Roma & Santa Maria Elisabetta on the Lido 🅣 041 2424 🅦 www.actv.it) and are the main form of transport for both locals and visitors. The buses zig-zag along the Grand Canal and other routes, stopping at alternate banks. Be aware that buses heading in both directions use the same stops.

Buses are regular and reliable, with the next departure time displayed on electronic screens at bus stations and a timetable available from the website. There is space for around 200 people on a water bus. Access is step-free so unless it is very crowded there is usually no problem for disabled travellers or those with prams or heavy luggage.

The most useful buses are nos. 1 and 82, which take around 30 minutes to travel up and down the Grand Canal. Several buses travel

⬤ *Water taxis are convenient, but expensive*

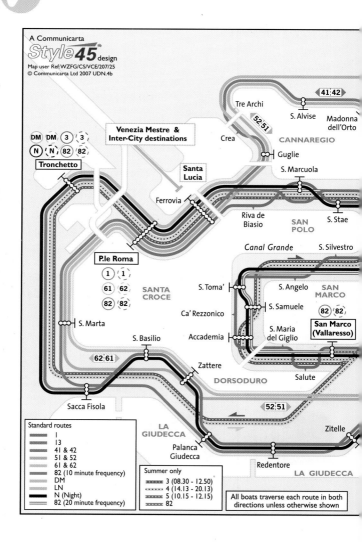

A Communicarta
Style45 design
Map user Ref: WZFG/CS/VCE/207/25
© Communicarta Ltd 2007 UDN.4b

Venezia Mestre &
Inter-City destinations

Tronchetto

Santa
Lucia

Tre Archi

S. Alvise

Madonna
dell'Orto

CANNAREGIO

Crea

Guglie

S. Marcuola

Ferrovia

Riva de
Biasio

SAN
POLO

S. Stae

Canal Grande

S. Silvestro

P.le Roma

SANTA
CROCE

S. Toma'

S. Angelo

SAN
MARCO

S. Marta

Ca' Rezzonico

S. Samuele

S. Basilio

Accademia

S. Maria
del Giglio

San Marco
(Vallaresso)

Zattere

Salute

DORSODURO

Sacca Fisola

Zitelle

LA
GIUDECCA

Palanca
Giudecca

Redentore

LA GIUDECCA

Standard routes

	1
	13
	41 & 42
	51 & 52
	61 & 62
	82 (10 minute frequency)
	DM
	LN
	N (Night)
	82 (20 minute frequency)

Summer only

	3 (08.30 - 12.50)
	4 (14.13 - 20.13)
	5 (10.15 - 12.15)
	82

All boats traverse each route in both
directions unless otherwise shown

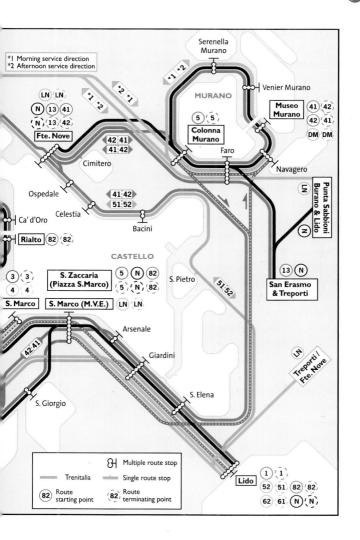

*1 Morning service direction
*2 Afternoon service direction

up the smaller canals or to the islands; stops are marked on the map on pages 56–7. A limited night bus service operates after midnight.

Single tickets lasting one hour can be bought in advance from an ACTV office or newsagent, at some boat stops, or on board. You can also purchase more economical one-day or three-day tickets that allow unlimited travel. The Venice Card (see page 22) includes unlimited public transport within the city. If you buy it in advance or at the airport it can also include the Alilaguna airport transfer boat.

Motoscafi (water taxis) take up to 12 passengers. Taxi ranks are situated at Piazzale Roma, Santa Lucia railway station, near the Rialto water bus stop, next to St Mark's Square, at the Valaresso water bus stop and at Giardini ex Reali. You can also hail water taxis or order one from your hotel, although hotels will often charge a ten percent booking fee. Even short journeys can be very expensive, with a minimum charge of €70 and a €10 surcharge after midnight, and must be paid for in cash. Always confirm a price with the driver before boarding. See ⓦ www.venezianamotoscafi.it for more information.

There are over 400 bridges in Venice but only three over the Grand Canal. A fourth 'Calatrava' bridge is currently under construction between Piazzale Roma and the railway station. To cross the Grand Canal you can take a *traghetto*, which costs €0.50 per person per crossing with standing room only.

CAR HIRE

All car hire offices are situated at the Piazzale Roma bus terminal.
Avis ❶ 041 523 7377 ⓦ www.avisautonoleggio.it
Europcar ❶ 041 523 8616 ⓦ www.europcar.it
Hertz ❶ 041 528 4091 ⓦ www.hertz.com

---

❶ *The famous Bridge of Sighs*

THE CITY OF
Venice

San Marco & Castello

Piazza San Marco (St Mark's Square) was described by Napoleon as 'the drawing room of Europe'. It has been the heart of the city for more than a millennium and is packed with fascinating buildings and attractions. The Castello district to the east is usually quieter than other central areas and is worth a visit for its churches of Santa Maria Formosa (see page 68) and Santi Giovanni e Paolo (see page 69). If you need a break from sightseeing pop into the small **Giardinetti Reali** (Royal Gardens ⏱ 09.00–18.00), originally built for Napoleon. Or head for the **Giardini Pubblici** (Public Gardens ⓐ Viale dei Giardini Pubblici, Castello ⏱ 08.30–20.00 (summer); 08.30–17.30 (winter) ⓦ Water bus to Giardini), the main site of the Biennale festival and one of Venice's few green spaces. It is a tranquil area and a good place to take a break in the shade away from the crowds and bustle. For some liquid refreshment go for a drink in the reputed **Hotel Danieli** (ⓐ Castello 4196, Riva degli Schiavoni ⓣ 041 522 64 80 ⓦ www.starwoodhotels.com ⏱ roof terrace bar: 15.00–18.00; lobby bar: 09.30–01.00 ⓦ Water bus to San Zaccaria) and gaze down at the lagoon from the roof terrace.

SIGHTS & ATTRACTIONS

Basilica di San Marco (St Mark's Basilica)

This stunning basilica was originally constructed in the 9th century to house the remains of St Mark, Venice's patron saint, and used to be the private chapel of the *doges*. What you see today mostly dates from the end of the 11th century. The exterior mosaics date mostly from the 17th and 18th centuries, with only one 13th-century original over the north door.

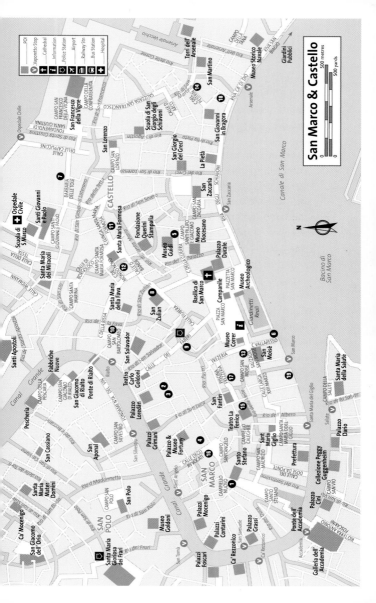

San Marco & Castello

POI

- Vaporetto Stop
- Cathedral
- Information
- Police Station
- Airport
- Railway Stn
- Bus Station
- Hospital

0   500 metres
0   500 yards

Canale di San Marco

Bacino di San Marco

N

AROUND PIAZZA SAN MARCO

At the eastern end of Piazza San Marco is the Basilica di San Marco (St Mark's Basilica). Next to it is the Palazzo Ducale (Doge's Palace) and opposite is the Campanile (Bell Tower) from which you can get excellent views of the city.

At the northern end is the Procuratie Vecchie, originally dating from the 12th century, but rebuilt after a fire in the 16th century. It used to house the offices of Venice's powerful magistrates and now contains the well-known **Quadri** café (📧 San Marco 121, Piazza San Marco ☎ 041 522 2105 🌐 www.quadrivenice.com 🕐 09.00–23.30, Apr–Oct; 09.00–23.30 Tues–Sun, Nov–Mar), which dates back to 1775. Just along from the Quadri is the Torre dell'Orologio, Venice's heavily embellished Renaissance clock tower. The arch beneath it leads to the Mercerie, Venice's main shopping area.

On the south side of the square is the legendary **Caffè Florian** (📧 San Marco 56, Piazza San Marco ☎ 041 520 5641 🌐 www.caffeflorian.com 🕐 10.00–00.00, May-Oct; 10.00–00.00 Thur–Tue, Nov–Apr) with its classic wood-panelled and mirrored interiors, originally opened in 1720 as a club for writers and artists. Both the Florian and the Quadri cafés have live classical music and, although expensive, are big tourist draws. It is part of experiencing the atmosphere of St Mark's Square to have a coffee or glass of wine at one of them.

The western end is the newest part of the square and houses the Correr Museum and the Ala Napoleonica.

The building's design is based on a basilica in Constantinople and Byzantine influences are evident in the elaborate domes and in the 4,000 sq m (40,000 sq ft) of mosaics inside.

Built in the shape of a Greek cross, the vast interior contains several chapels, as well as a baptistry, museum and treasury. The treasury contains a stunning collection of Byzantine gold and silver spoils, including chandeliers and chalices. The most spectacular of all is the Pala d'Oro, a gorgeous, gold and gem-encrusted altarpiece, made in Constantinople in 976. It used to be covered by the Pala Feriale, a panel painted by Paolo Veneziano and now on display in the basilica.

If you climb the stairway you'll find four gilded copper horses overlooking the square – a great photo opportunity. The horses, a symbol of Venice, are thought to be Greek or Roman in origin and were part of the plunder brought back from Constantinople in 1204. The horses outside the building are replicas but the originals are protected inside the basilica.

The chancel is separated from the rest of the church by a red marble choir screen. You can access it via the San Clemente chapel and it is worth admiring its intricate mosaic depicting St Mark's body being transported to Venice.

❶ Luggage and rucksacks are not allowed in the basilica. You can leave your bags safely at Ateneo San Basso, a three minute walk to the left of the main entrance (❸ Calle San Basso 315A). ❸ Piazza San Marco ❶ 041 522 5205 ⏱ 09.45–17.30 Mon–Sat, 14.00–16.00 Sun, May–Sept; 09.45–16.30 Mon–Sat, 14.00–16.00 Sun, Oct–Apr ⛴ Water bus to Valaresso. Admission charge for treasury, loggia, Museo Marciano, chancel and Pala d'Oro. Main basilica free of charge.

PHOENIX FROM THE FLAMES

To the west of St Mark's Square is the famous 18th-century opera house of La Fenice, which means 'The Phoenix'. The name derives from this legendary animal's cycle of death and rebirth. The opera house burned down in 1774, was reopened in 1792, but was subsequently destroyed by fire in 1836. Repaired and reopened again, the interior was heavily damaged by yet another fire in 1996. It was eventually fully restored at the end of 2003, with new stages, state-of-the-art equipment and a new roof, and hopefully this time with improved fire protection. Book well in advance for excellent opera, ballet and concert performances. ❸ San Marco 1965, Campo San Fantin ❶ 041 940 200 ❿ www.teatrolafenice.it ❷ Water bus to Valaresso

Campanile (Bell Tower)

This 100 m (330 ft) red brick tower is the tallest building in Venice and one of the city's most prominent landmarks. It was originally built in the 9th century but took its current shape in 1514. It collapsed in 1902 but was rebuilt ten years later. You can take a lift to the top and enjoy great views of the city on a clear day. Go early if possible to avoid long queues. ❸ Piazza San Marco ❶ 041 522 4064 ❶ 09.00–19.00, Apr–June & Sept–Oct; 09.00–21.00, July & Aug; 09.30–16.15, Nov–Mar; last entry one hour before closing ❷ Water bus to Valaresso. Admission charge

Ospedale Civile (City Hospital)

The city's main hospital in the Castello district has an astounding marble façade on account of its previous role as home to one of

Venice's wealthy philanthropic *scuole*. Ask at reception to visit the library on the first floor to see a fine 16th-century carved wooden ceiling and some interesting paintings. The hospital chapel, the Church of San Lazzaro dei Mendicanti, has an early Tintoretto and a Veronese and is also open to the public. The imposing equestrian statue by Verrochio just outside is of Bartolomeo Colleoni, the 15th-century mercenary commander. ⓐ Castello 6777, Campo Santi Giovanni e Paolo ⓣ 041 529 4111 ⓛ Library: 08.30–14.00 Mon–Fri; Chapel: 08.00–12.00 Mon–Sat, 09.00-10.00 Sun

Palazzo Ducale (Doge's Palace)

Originally constructed in the 9th century as a fortress but subsequently destroyed by fire, the present Gothic building dates from the 14th

The Scuola Grande di San Marco serves as the city hospital's façade

and 15th centuries. The building was the seat of the city's government and *doges* were ceremonially crowned at the top of the Scala dei Giganti (Giant's Staircase).

As you go on, admire the impressive entrance Porta della Carta, leading to a courtyard. Inside, you will find huge and richly decorated chambers, many with fine paintings by masters such as Tintoretto and Veronese. Look out for Tintoretto's *Paradise* in the Sala del Maggiore Consiglio (Hall of the Great Council). The Ponte dei Sospiri (Bridge of Sighs) leads to the prison, which you can also visit.

It is well worth taking a 'Secret Itineraries' tour to appreciate the best of the art on display, which you can book up to two days in advance at the *palazzo* or by phone. It is fun for children as well as adults and there are regular English-language tours lasting 90 minutes. ⓐ San Marco 1 ⓣ 041 520 9070 ⓦ www.museiciviciveneziani.it ⓛ 09.00–19.00, Apr–Oct; 09.00–17.00, Nov–Mar ⓝ Water bus to Valaresso. Admission charge

Palazzo Grassi

This neo-classical *palazzo* on the Grand Canal, one of the last to be built before the fall of the Venetian Republic, was designed by Giorgio Massari in 1749 around a large colonnaded courtyard. It was recently bought by French tycoon François Pinault and the interior has been remodelled by Japanese architect Tadao Ando. Selections from Pinault's vast collection of modern art are on display in the building, along with exhibitions of specially commissioned work. With around 200 works on show at a time it is an exciting destination for lovers of modern art. Check the website for exhibition details. ⓐ San Marco 3231, Campo San Samuele ⓣ 041 523 1680 ⓦ www.palazzograssi.it ⓛ 10.00–19.00; last entry one hour before closing ⓝ Water bus to San Samuele. Admission charge

Piazzetta San Marco

In front of the Doge's Palace is an area called the Piazzetta containing two granite pillars topped with winged lions, the symbol of Venice. Dating from the 12th century, the columns marked the entrance to Venice at a time when you could only arrive at the city by sea. From the Piazzetta you can see the islands of San Giorgio and Giudecca and the church of Santa Maria Della Salute at the end of the Grand Canal. The Grand Canal meanders through Venice's streets for around 4 km (2.5 miles) in an 's' shape and is the city's main artery, with magnificent *palazzi* and museums along its length.

San Zaccaria

This church dating back to the 9th century is named after St Zacharias, father of John the Baptist, whose remains are allegedly enshrined in the second altar on the right.

The church's impressive façade was designed by Mauro Codussi in 1515. The bell tower was built in the 13th century, and the lower part of the façade is Gothic, dating from the late 15th century. The interior

ARSENALE

While you are in Castello take the chance to stroll around the vast walled Arsenale complex. Dating from the 12th century, it was once the world's greatest shipyard and essential to Venice's naval might. It is largely closed to the public as it is still a naval headquarters but it is worth admiring its imposing exterior wall. During the Biennale festivals (see page 9) some of its buildings are opened up as exhibition and theatre spaces (🅐 Campo dell'Arsenale 🅝 Water bus to Arsenale).

THE CITY

is large and dark, a mixture of Gothic and Renaissance styles, though the crypt was part of the 9th-century church. The walls of the nave are covered with huge late 17th-century baroque paintings.

The highlight of the church is Giovanni Bellini's *Madonna and Child and Four Saints* (1505), displayed over the second altar on the left. The chapels of St Athanasius and St Tarasius contain several paintings, including works by Tintoretto, Van Dyck, Giandomenico Tiepolo, as well as polyptychs painted by Antonio Vivarini in 1443. ❸ Castello 4693, Campo San Zaccaria ❶ 041 522 1257 ● 10.00–12.00 & 16.00–18.00 Mon–Sat, 16.00–18.00 Sun ◑ Water bus to San Zaccaria. Admission charge for chapels

Santa Maria Formosa

This church, situated in one of the liveliest and largest squares in Venice, is worth seeing if only for the grotesque faces on the baroque

◗ *St Mark's Basilica*

bell tower. The present church was designed by Mauro Codussi in the late 15th century. It has two façades, one facing the canal and the other facing the square. Inside are works by Palma il Vecchio and Bartolomeo Vivarini. **ⓐ** Castello 5263, Campo Santa Maria Formosa **ⓣ** 041 275 0462 **ⓦ** www.chorusvenezia.org **ⓛ** 10.00–17.00 Mon–Sat **ⓝ** Water bus to San Zaccaria. Admission charge

Santi Giovanni e Paolo (Church of Saint John and Saint Paul)

Also known as San Zanipolo, this church is one of the largest and most important in the city. It was originally built in the Gothic style for the Dominicans and consecrated in the early 15th century. The doorway is one of the earliest examples of the Renaissance style in Venice; there are other Renaissance features inside along with a Baroque high altar. Despite this mixture of styles, the church is remarkable for its general unity. It was second only to St Mark's Basilica in Venice's public life and contains fine monuments to no fewer than 25 *doges*.

Worth seeking out are the Capella del Rosario (Chapel of the Rosary) for its paintings by Veronese, and the chapel of San Domenico for its ceiling. There is a lovely polyptych (1464) by Giovanni Bellini at the second altar on the right. **ⓐ** Castello 6363, Campo SS Giovanni e Paolo **ⓣ** 041 523 5913 **ⓛ** 07.30–13.30 & 15.30–19.00 **ⓝ** Water bus to Ospedale. Admission charge

Santo Stefano

Along one side of the lively Campo Santo Stefano, also sometimes known as the Campo Francesco Morosini after the 17th-century *doge* who lived in the square, is the church of Santo Stefano. It is worth popping in to see its graceful Gothic interior and sumptuous red and white decoration. Built in the 14th and 15th centuries for the Augustinians, its ceiling is in the shape of ship's keel. You can also

see works by Tintoretto in the sacristy. ⓐ San Marco 2774, Campo
Santo Stefano ❶ 041 275 0462 ⓦ www.chorusvenezia.org ❶ 10.00–17.00
Mon–Sat Ⓝ Water bus to San Samuele. Admission charge

CULTURE

Museo Correr & Museo Archeologico
(Correr & Archaeological Museums)

The Correr Museum, a celebration of Venice's rich art and history,
is housed in the Procuratie Nuove at the western end of St Mark's
Square and entered through the Ala Napoleonica.

The first few rooms contain historical artefacts and works by
Antonio Canova, arguably Venice's greatest sculptor. The real treat
is on the second floor, where you can wander around the Quaderia
picture gallery to get an excellent overview of Venetian art and its
development. Look out for Carpaccio's *Portrait of a Young Man in
a Red Hat* and his *Two Venetian Ladies*. There are also paintings by
Jacopo Bellini and his more celebrated sons Giovanni and Gentile.

Your ticket to the Correr Museum also entitles you to visit the
Archaeological Museum. It contains Greek, Roman and Babylonian
antiquities, including sculptures from Greece and Rome which
influenced Venetian artists. ⓐ Piazza San Marco 52 ❶ 041 240 5211
ⓦ www.museicivicivenziani.it ❶ 09.00–19.00, Apr–Oct;
09.00–17.00, Nov–Mar; last entry one hour before closing
Ⓝ Water bus to Valaresso. Admission charge

Museo Fortuny (Fortuny Museum)

This crumbling 15th-century house, originally the Palazzo Pesaro
degli Orfei, was the home of Spanish fashion designer, painter and
photographer Mariano Fortuny. It was left to the city by his widow

● *The hidden treasure of the Fortuny Museum*

in 1956 and is currently under long-term restoration work.
Al three floors remain open throughout the restoration period,
which will continue for the foreseeable future, with the museum
displaying high quality photographic and other exhibitions.
🅐 San Marco 3780, Campo San Benedetto 🅣 041 520 0995
🅦 www.museicivicivenziani.it 🅝 Water bus to Sant'Angelo
🅛 10.00–18.00 Tues–Sun. Admission charge

Museo Storico Navale (Naval History Museum)

Set over four floors in a former granary near the Arsenale, this well
laid-out museum features displays on the history of the Venetian
and Italian navies. Other exhibits based around Venice's long and
fruitful relationship with the sea include a room devoted to the
gondola and an impressive collection of sea shells. Great for children
as well as adults. 🅐 Castello 2148, Riva San Biagio 🅣 041 520 0276
🅛 08.45–13.30 Mon–Fri, 08.45–13.00 Sat 🅝 Water bus to Arsenale.
Admission charge

Scuola di San Giorgio degli Schiavoni

The Venetian *scuole*, mainly founded in the 17th century, were
charitable societies formed by laymen who had the same background
or profession. Many of these societies were very wealthy and their
impressive buildings house some of the city's finest art works.

The Scuola di San Giorgio degli Schiavoni, founded in the
15th century by Venice's increasingly powerful community of Slavs,
is one of the smallest of the many *scuole* in the city but arguably
the most enjoyable to visit. The rectangular ground floor is wood
panelled and contains a cycle of richly coloured and animated
paintings by Vittore Carpaccio depicting the life of St George,
St Tryphon and St Jerome. Make sure you look up to admire the

wooden ceiling. A staircase lined with paintings leads to the upper hall, also wood panelled, which has a gilded wooden ceiling further decorated by oval paintings. ⓐ Castello 3259A, Calle dei Furlani ⓣ 041 522 8828 ⓛ 09.30–12.30 & 15.30–18.30 Tues–Sat, 15.30–18.30 Sun, Apr–Oct; 10.00–12.30 & 15.00–18.00 Tues–Sat, 10.00–12.30 Sun, Nov–Mar ⓦ Water bus to San Zaccaria. Admission charge

RETAIL THERAPY

Araba Fenice Leading fashion boutique with exclusive designs. ⓐ San Marco 1822, Frezzaria ⓣ 041 522 0664 ⓛ 09.30–13.00 & 15.30–19.30 Mon–Sat ⓦ Water bus to Valaresso

Arnaldo Battois This designer store offers an exclusive selection of garments in luxurious fabrics. ⓐ San Marco 4271, Calle dei Fuseri ⓣ 041 528 5944 ⓦ www.arnoldoebattois.com ⓛ 10.00–19.30 Mon–Sat ⓦ Water bus to Rialto

Attombri Two local brothers create contemporary necklaces and bracelets from antique Venetian glass beads. ⓐ San Marco 2668A, Campo San Maurizio ⓣ 041 521 0789 ⓛ 09.30–13.00 & 14.30–19.00 Mon–Sat ⓦ Water bus to Giglio

Bevilacqua One of the best shops for fine textiles. ⓐ San Marco 337B, Ponte della Canonica ⓣ 041 528 7581 ⓛ 10.00–19.00 Mon–Sat, 09.30–17.00 Sun ⓦ Water bus to Valaresso

Guess Jeans This swish new chain store holds the complete Guess range for men and women. ⓐ San Marco 4596, Calle del Carbon

☎ 041 241 1494 **🌐** www.guess.com **🕐** 09.30–19.30 Mon–Sat,
11.00–19.30 Sun **⌾** Water bus to Rialto

Il Papiro Stationery and attractive boxes made of marbled paper.
◎ San Marco 2764, Calle del Piovan **☎** 041 522 3055 **🕐** 10.00–19.30
or **◎** Castello 5275, Calle delle Bande **☎** 041 522 3648 **🕐** 10.30–19.00
⌾ Water bus to Valaresso

Il Prato One of the city's best glass shops. **◎** San Marco 2457, Calle de
le Ostreghe **☎** 041 523 1148 **🕐** 10.00–19.30 Mon–Sat, 11.00–19.00 Sun
🌐 www.ilpratovenezia.com **⌾** Water bus to Giglio

⬤ *Window-shopping in Venice's fashionable Mercerie Street*

Jesurum High quality lace and linen. ❸ San Marco 4857, Merceria del Capitello ❶ 041 520 6177 🕐 09.30–19.30 Mon–Sat, 10.30–18.30 Sun Ⓝ Water bus to Valaresso

Ottico Fabbricatore Stylish store selling designer eyewear, cashmere and leather bags. ❸ San Marco 4773, Calle dell'Ovo ❶ 041 522 5263 Ⓦ www.otticofabbricatore.com 🕐 09.00–12.30 & 15.30–19.30 Mon–Sat Ⓝ Water bus to Rialto

Papier Mâché This workshop produces unusual paper creations using traditional techniques. ❸ Castello 5175, Calle Lunga Santa Maria Formosa ❶ 041 522 9995 Ⓦ www.papiermache.it 🕐 09.00–19.30 Mon–Sat, 10.00–19.00 Sun Ⓝ Water bus to Rialto

Peletteria Silvia Beautifully crafted shoes and quality bags in the softest leather and suede. ❸ San Marco 4466 ❶ 041 523 5749 🕐 09.00–19.30 Mon–Sat Ⓝ Water bus to Rialto

TAKING A BREAK

All' Angolo £ ❶ Popular café serving sandwiches and snacks. ❸ San Marco 3464, Campo Santo Stefano ❶ 041 522 0710 🕐 06.30–23.00 (summer); 06.30–21.00 (winter) Ⓝ Water bus to San Samuele

Andrea Zanin £ ❷ Owner Andrea produces delectable pastries, with miniature versions for the calorie-conscious. Small pizzas and savoury pastries also available. ❸ San Marco 4589, Campo San Luca ❶ 041 522 4803 🕐 07.30–20.00 Mon–Sat, 10.30–19.30 Sun Ⓝ Water bus to Rialto

Leon Bianco £ ❸ Good value hot dishes and great toasted sandwiches. **Ⓐ** San Marco 4153, Salizzada San Luca **Ⓣ** 041 522 1180 **Ⓛ** 08.00–22.00 Mon–Sat **Ⓦ** Water bus to Rialto

Teamo £ ❹ Hip new lounge-bar with an excellent range of light meals and wines. **Ⓐ** San Marco 3795, Rio Terrà della Mandola **Ⓣ** 0347 366 5016 **Ⓦ** www.teamo.it **Ⓛ** 08.00–22.00 Mon–Sat **Ⓦ** Water bus to Sant'Angelo

All' Aciugheta £–££ ❺ Restaurant, bar and café set in a tiny square, offering wine, snacks, pizzas and full meals. **Ⓐ** Castello 4357, Campo Santi Fillipo e Giacomo **Ⓣ** 041 522 4292 **Ⓛ** 11.00–24.00 **Ⓦ** Water bus to San Zaccaria

Harry's Bar £££ ❻ The place to see and be seen. Food is expensive but good and portions are large. Pop in for an impeccably served sandwich or splash out on a cocktail. **Ⓐ** San Marco 1323, Calle Vallaresso **Ⓣ** 041 528 57 77 **Ⓛ** 10.30–23.00 **Ⓦ** Water bus to Valaresso

AFTER DARK

The area around San Marco is surprisingly quiet late in the evening, and Castello is emptier still. Most restaurants close by 22.00.

RESTAURANTS & WINE BARS
Bandierette £ ❼ Excellent value lunch or dinner in this low-key restaurant. **Ⓐ** Castello 6671, Barbaria delle Tole **Ⓣ** 041 522 0619 **Ⓛ** 12.00–14.00 & 19.00–22.00 Wed–Sun, 12.00–14.00 Mon **Ⓦ** www.bandierette.it **Ⓦ** Water bus to Ospedale

Cavatappi £ ❽ Wine bar serving tasty snacks during the day and fuller meals in the evening. ❸ San Marco 525, Campo della Guerra ❶ 041 296 0252 ❹ 11.00–21.00 Tues–Sat, 11.00–15.00 Sun ⓝ Water bus to Valaresso

A la Campana £–££ ❾ Good traditional food in a rustic atmosphere. Popular with locals for both lunch and dinner. ❸ San Marco 4720, Calle dei Fabbri ❶ 041 528 5170 ❹ 12.00–15.00 & 19.00–22.00 Mon–Sat ⓝ Water bus to Rialto

Alla Botte £–££ ❿ Lively wine bar with a restaurant serving simple, reasonably priced pasta and local dishes. You can also get snacks at the bar all day. ❸ San Marco 5482, Campo San Bartolomeo ❶ 041 520 9775

● *Soak up the atmosphere in the cafés on St Mark's Square*

🕐 12.00–15.00 & 19.00–22.00 Mon–Wed, Fri & Sat, 12.00–15.00 Sun; closed July 🚤 Water bus to Rialto

Alla Mascareta ££ ⑪ Popular, unpretentious wine bar with simple but tasty food. One of the few late-opening bars around. 🏠 Castello 5183, Calle Lunga Santa Maria Formosa 📞 041 523 0744 🕐 19.00–02.00 Fri–Tues 🚤 Water bus to San Zaccaria

Alle Testiere ££ ⑫ This small restaurant specialises in fish and seafood subtly flavoured with herbs and spices. 🏠 Castello 5801, Calle del Mondo Novo 📞 041 522 7220 🕐 12.00–14.00 & 19.00–22.30, Tues–Sat 🚤 Water bus to San Zaccaria

Bacaro ££ ⑬ A fashionable late-opening bar and restaurant, with pricey but good-quality food. 🏠 San Marco 1345, Salizada San Moisè 📞 041 296 0687 🕐 09.00–02.00 🚤 Water bus to Valaresso

Corte Sconta ££ ⑭ Simple, popular restaurant with a courtyard specialising in fish and seafood. 🏠 Castello 3886, Calle del Pestrin 📞 041 522 70 24 🕐 12.30–14.00 & 19.00–21.30 Tues–Sat; closed Jan & mid July–mid Aug 🚤 Water bus to Arsenale

Vino Vino ££ ⑮ This wine bar is attached to Antico Martini, one of Venice's oldest restaurants, and has established itself as one of Venice's best for both food and wine. 🏠 San Marco 2007A, Calle della Veste 📞 041 241 7688 🕐 11.30–23.30 🌐 www.vinovino.co.it 🚤 Water bus to Valaresso or Giglio

Acqua Pazza ££–£££ ⑯ A favoured place for sitting out in the square under awnings. Excellent southern Italian pizzas and

pasta but the service receives mixed reports. ⓐ San Marco 3808,
Campo Sant'Angelo ⓒ 12.30–14.00 & 19.00–21.30 Tues–Sun
Ⓝ Water bus to Sant'Angelo

Centrale ££–£££ ⑰ Trendy late-opening lounge bar and
restaurant with stylish décor and low lighting. Regular live music.
ⓐ San Marco 1659 B, Piscina Frezzeria ⓣ 041 296 0664 ⓒ 18.30–02.00
Ⓦ www.centrale-lounge.com Ⓝ Water bus to Valaresso

Al Covo £££ ⑱ One of the best restaurants in Venice,
well known for its excellent fish and meat dishes served in
comfortable surroundings. ⓐ Castello 3968, Campiello della
Pescaria ⓣ 041 522 3812 ⓒ 12.45–15.00 & 19.30–22.00 Fri–Tues
Ⓝ Water bus to Arsenale

La Cusina £££ ⑲ Hotel restaurant on the Grand Canal serving
inventive dishes based on fresh local produce, particularly fish.
For a romantic meal book the table on the small jetty.
ⓐ Hotel Europa & Regina, San Marco 2159 ⓣ 041 240 0001
ⓒ 12.30–14.30 & 19.30–22.30 Ⓝ Water bus to Valaresso

ENTERTAINMENT

Two of Venice's best theatres, La Fenice opera house (see page 64)
and Teatro Carlo Goldoni (see page 22), are in this area. Otherwise,
evening entertainment is based around the restaurants and the
orchestras at the Quadri and Florian cafés (see page 62). For late-
night cocktails and music, you can try **Bar Aurora** ⓐ San Marco 49,
Piazza San Marco ⓣ 041 528 6405 ⓒ 08.30–02.00, Mar–Oct;
08.30–02.00 Wed–Mon, Nov–Feb Ⓝ Water bus to Valaresso

Dorsoduro

The popular district of Dorsoduro, just across the Accademia Bridge, contains three of Venice's best museums – the Accademia with its fine collection of Venetian art, the Ca' Rezzonico with its focus on 18th-century Venice, and the Peggy Guggenheim Collection of contemporary art. There are also several fine churches. The area is young and lively, filled with students and visitors. Walking along the Grand Canal section of Dorsoduro gives you a different perspective on the magnificent façades of the San Marco side.

Most of the area's sights, small galleries and craft shops are in the eastern part, many lining the Grand Canal. The far western part is a working-class dock area, some of which is now being redeveloped. At the far eastern end of Dorsoduro is the vast 17th-century *dogana*, or customs house, which will hopefully soon be converted into an art gallery. South of the Grand Canal is the quayside of Zattere, one of the most relaxing and attractive places in Venice in which to have lunch or a drink. Here you get a view of the island of Giudecca and can watch the local rowing clubs practising. Other good places to relax are the Campo Santa Margherita or Campo San Barnaba, two of Venice's liveliest squares.

SIGHTS & ATTRACTIONS

Gesuati (Santa Maria del Rosario)

Walk along the Zattere quayside and pay a quick visit to this striking church, designed by Giorgio Massari and completed in 1735. It faces Palladio's church of Il Redentore on the island of Giudecca (see page 123) and its façade is a deliberate reflection of the other

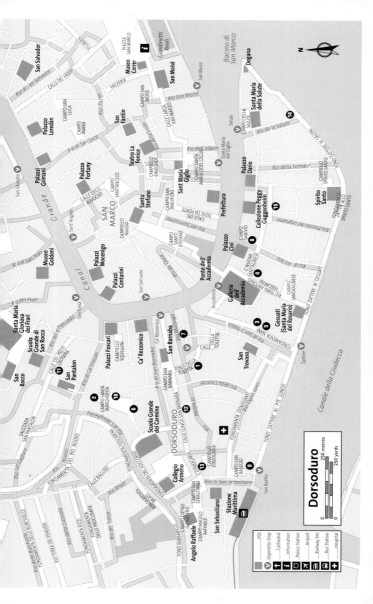

church. Inside, look out for the theatrical sculptures by Giovanni Morlaiter and for Giambattista Tiepolo's ceiling frescoes.

ⓐ Dorsoduro 917, Fondamenta della Zattere ai Gesuati ⓣ 041 523 0625 ⓦ www.chorusvenezia.org ⓛ 10.00–17.00 Mon–Sat ⓝ Water bus to Zattere. Admission charge

Santa Maria della Salute

Dominating the entrance to the Grand Canal, this domed church with its gorgeously carved baroque façade is an instantly recognisable symbol of Venice. *Salute* means 'health', and the church was built in thanksgiving after the end of a terrible plague in 1630 which killed a third of the city's population. It is the centre of the yearly Festa della Salute celebrations on 21 November, in which thanks-givers

🔺 *You can't help but admire Santa Maria della Salute*

walk across a temporary pontoon bridge from the Gritti Palace hotel to the church and street vendors mingle with the crowds selling candy floss, balloons and votive candles.

The church was designed by architect Baldassare Longhena but remained unfinished until 1687, five years after Longhena's death. Given the grandeur of the exterior, the interior is surprisingly muted, although the marble floor stands out. One altar contains Titian's *Descent of the Holy Spirit* (1550). The best paintings are in the sacristy, including Titian's early altarpiece *Saint Mark Enthroned with Saints* (1512) and Tintoretto's *Wedding at Cana* (1551). ❸ Campo della Salute ❶ 041 274 39 11 ❺ 09.00–12.00 & 15.00–18.00 ❻ Water bus to Salute. Admission charge for sacristy

San Sebastiano

The 16th-century church of San Sebastiano is the best place to see the sumptuous work of Paolo Veronese (1528–88). The painter moved to Venice as a young man and lived and died near the church, where he was later buried. His luminous ceiling paintings depict the lives of Esther and St Sebastian. The unity of the decoration and the radiance of Veronese's style make the church's interior one of the most beautiful in Venice. ❸ Dorsoduro 1686, Campo San Sebastiano ❶ 041 275 0462 ❿ www.chorusvenezia.org ❺ 10.00–17.00 Mon–Sat ❻ Water bus to San Basilio. Admission charge

CULTURE

Ca' Rezzonico

Here is the place to get an idea of the splendour in which the wealthiest Venetians once lived. This baroque *palazzo*, designed in 1667 by Baldassare Longhena for the wealthy Bon family, was

subsequently sold to the wealthy Rezzonico family. It was bought
by the son of poet Robert Browning, who died in the house in 1889.
It has been a museum since 1936.

The building's splendid decorative features include massive
chandeliers, fine carved furniture, tapestries, ceilings painted by
Giambattista Tiepolo and frescoes by Giandomenico Tiepolo.
The architectural highlight is Giorgio Massari's magnificent ballroom
with its gilded wood and *trompe l'oeil* paintings.

In the gallery on the second floor are two rare Canaletto paintings
along with 18th-century scenes of Venetian life by Francesco Guardi
and Pietro Longhi. On the third floor is a reconstructed 18th-century
pharmacy. Make sure you take time to admire the view from the
upper floors. ❸ Dorsoduro 3136, Fondamenta Rezzonico ❶ 041 410 0100
Ⓦ www.museiciviciv250eneziani.it ❺ 10.00–18.00 Wed–Mon, Apr–Oct;
10.00–17.00 Wed–Mon, Nov–Mar ◎ Water bus to Ca' Rezzonico.
Admission charge

Galleria dell'Accademia (Accademia Gallery)

The Accademia Gallery is arguably one of the world's greatest art
galleries. The collection was begun in 1750 and greatly expanded in
1807 under the orders of Napoleon, who confiscated works of art
from churches and other religious institutions to put on display
in the museum. The building is currently under restoration and
expected to be fully reopened in 2009, but many of the 24 rooms
should stay open during the refurbishment.

The galleries, mostly arranged chronologically, contain early
Byzantine-influenced works and slightly later Gothic devotional works
including paintings by Paolo Veneziano. Early Renaissance works by
Giovanni Bellini and Vittore Carpaccio follow, but the highlight for
most visitors is the superb collection of high Renaissance art including

ACCADEMIA BRIDGE

To reach the Accademia from Campo Santo Stefano you will cross a busy wooden bridge known as the Accademia Bridge. Originally built in cast iron in 1854, it was later demolished for being too low. A wooden bridge was erected as a temporary structure in 1932 and replaced with a stronger replica in 1984. Standing on the bridge will give you some great views of the Grand Canal.

⬤ *Take a stroll over the famous Accademia Bridge*

paintings by masters such as Titian, Tintoretto, Veronese, Giorgione and Mantegna. Look out for Titian's *St John the Baptist* (1535) and his final *Pietà* (1576), for Veronese's huge *Feast in the House of Levi* (1573) and Tintoretto's dark and dramatic *Translation of the Body of St Mark* (1562) and *Miracle of the Slave* (1548). Other paintings not to miss are Lorenzo Lotto's sensitive *Portrait of a Gentleman* (1525) and Giorgione's wonderfully enigmatic *The Tempest* (1507).

A GONDOLA TO THE GUGGENHEIM

The Peggy Guggenheim Collection is one of Venice's most popular art museums, containing a fantastic collection of contemporary works.

Peggy Guggenheim (1898–1979) moved into the Palazzo Venier dei Leoni on the Grand Canal in 1949. The building itself, with its low Istrian stone façade and small garden, was begun in 1748 but remains unfinished. Peggy bequeathed the *palazzo* and her superb collection of modern art to the Solomon R Guggenheim Foundation, who formally inaugurated the museum the year after her death. The foundation also oversees museums in New York, Bilbao, Berlin and Las Vegas.

The art collection contains Cubist works by Braque, Picasso and Leger as well as paintings by surrealist artists such as Magritte, Dalí and Max Ernst. You can also admire a good collection of works by Paul Klee, Jackson Pollock and other abstract expressionists. The museum's most recognisable sculpture, a priapic rider with outstretched arms, is Marino Marini's *Angel of the City*.

The museum also offers visitors excellent views from the terrace, a pleasant sculpture garden, a bookshop and a good café. ❸ Dorsorduro 701, Palazzo Venier dei Leoni ☎ 041 240 54 11 🅦 www.guggenheim-venice.it 🕓 10.00–18.00 Wed–Mon 🚤 Water bus to Salute. Admission charge

Artists featured in the rest of the collection are Jacopo Bassano, Giambattista Tiepolo, Canaletto, Carpaccio and Bellini, whose paintings depict Venice in the 16th century. *The Life of St Ursula* (1590–5) by Carpaccio and Titian's outstanding *Presentation of the Virgin* (1538) are two other highlights of the museum. ⓐ Dorsoduro 1050, Campo Carita ⓣ 041 522 2247 ⓦ www.gallerieaccademia.org ⓛ 08.15–19.15 Tues–Sun, 09.00–14.00 Mon ⓦ Water bus to Accademia. Admission charge

🔺 *The Angel of the City, at the Guggenheim Museum*

San Pantalon

The exterior of this church is mundane, but step inside and be astonished by its remarkable illusionist ceiling depicting *The Martyrdom and Apotheosis of St Pantalon* by Gian Antonio Fumiani. The 40 canvases took Fumiani 24 years to complete from the start of his commission in 1680. ⓐ Dorsoduro 3765, Campo San Pantalon ⓘ 041 270 2464 ⓛ 15.00–18.00 Mon–Sat ⓦ Water bus to San Tomà

Scuola Grande dei Carmini

Baldasarre Longhena, famed architect of Santa Maria della Salute, was commissioned by the Carmelite order to build this *scuola* next to the church of Santa Maria dei Carmini in 1667. The highlights are Giambattista Tiepolo's nine characteristic ceiling paintings on the first floor. ⓐ Dorsoduro 2617, Campo dei Carmini ⓘ 041 528 9420 ⓛ 09.00–18.00 Mon–Sat, 09.00–16.00 Sun, Apr–Oct; 09.00–16.00 Mon–Sun, Nov–Mar ⓦ Water bus to Ca' Rezzonico. Admission charge

RETAIL THERAPY

3865 Fashionable women's clothing and accessories. ⓐ Dorsoduro 3749, Calle San Pantalon ⓘ 041 720 595 ⓛ 10.00–19.45 Tues–Sat ⓦ Water bus to San Tomà

Antichita Antique glass beads made into necklaces or bracelets while you wait. ⓐ Dorsoduro 1195, Calle Toletta ⓘ 041 522 3159 ⓛ 09.30–13.00 & 15.30–19.00 Mon–Sat ⓦ Water bus to Accademia

Carta Alta Mask shop with an excellent range of classy bags. ⓐ Dorsoduro 2808, Campo San Barnaba ⓘ 041 523 8313

Ⓦ www.venicemaskshop.com Ⓛ 10.30–14.30 & 15.30–19.30
Mon–Sat Ⓝ Water bus to Ca' Rezzonico

Il Canapé Sumptuous fabric and interior design store. Ⓐ Dorsoduro 3736,
Calle San Pantalon Ⓣ 041 714 264 Ⓦ www.ilcanape.it Ⓛ 09.00–12.45
& 15.15–19.30 Tue–Sat, 15.15–19.30 Mon Ⓝ Water bus to San Tomà

Il Pavone Attractive handmade paper products. Ⓐ Dorsoduro 721,
Fondamenta Venier dei Leoni Ⓣ 041 523 4517 Ⓛ 09.30–13.30
& 14.30–18.30 Ⓝ Water bus to Salute

Madera Contemporary tableware and other design objects.
Ⓐ Dorsoduro 2762, Campo San Barnaba Ⓣ 041 522 4181 Ⓛ 10.30–13.00
& 15.30–19.30 Mon–Sat Ⓝ Water bus to Ca' Rezzonico

Mondo Novo One of the city's best mask shops. Ⓐ Dorsoduro 3063,
Rio Terra Canal Ⓣ 041 528 7344 Ⓛ 09.00–18.30 Mon–Sat
Ⓝ Water bus to Ca' Rezzonico

Vintage a Go Go Retro clothing store selling vintage Pucci and
Armani. Ⓐ Calle Lunga San Barnaba Ⓣ 041 277 7895 Ⓛ 10.00–13.00
& 15.30–19.30 Mon–Sat Ⓝ Water bus to Ca' Rezzonico

TAKING A BREAK

The Zattere is great for relaxing in cafés and is one of the few places
in the city where you can picnic. For a more vibrant atmosphere and
cheaper food, make your way to the lively Campo Santa Margherita
or Campo San Barnaba.

Ai Artisti £ ❶ A simple stop for a drink or plate of pasta.
❸ Dorsoduro 1196A, Fondamenta della Toletta ❶ 041 523 8944
🕐 08.00–22.00 Mon–Sat Ⓝ Water bus to Accademia

Ai Do Draghi £ ❷ Good sandwiches, salads, wines and beers. Tables
outside. ❸ Dorsoduro 3665, Campo Santa Margherita ❶ 041 528 9731
🕐 07.30–02.00 (summer); 07.30–22.00 Fri–Wed (winter)
Ⓝ Water bus to Ca' Rezzonico

Cantinone gia Schiavi £ ❸ A comprehensive selection of local wines
and light bites. ❸ Dorsoduro 992, Ponte San Trovaso ❶ 041 523 0034
🕐 08.00–20.30 Mon–Sat Ⓝ Water bus to Zattere

Da Gino £ ❹ Popular with students, this café is good for coffee
and sandwiches. ❸ Dorsoduro 853A, Calle Nuova Sant'Agnese
🕐 06.00–19.30 Mon–Sat Ⓝ Water bus to Accademia

Gelateria Lo Squero £ ❺ Some of the best ice cream in Venice.
❸ Dorsoduro 989, Fondamenta Nani ❶ 041 241 3601 🕐 10.30–21.00
Ⓝ Water bus to Zattere

Orange £ ❻ Trendy modern champagne and wine bar with tables
outside, decorated in orange and popular with students. Good snacks,
coffee, cocktails and light meals. ❸ Dorsoduro 3054, Campo Santa
Margherita ❶ 041 523 4740 🕐 07.00– 02.00 Mon–Sat, 17.00–24.00 Sun
Ⓝ Water bus to Ca' Rezzonico

Osteria Vini Padovani £ ❼ Good-value eatery tucked behind the busy
Calle della Toletta. ❸ Dorsoduro, Calle dei Cerchieri ❶ 041 523 6370
🕐 07.00–23.00 Mon–Sat Ⓝ Water bus to Accademia

Vecio Forner £ ❽ Bar serving excellent coffee, sandwiches, snacks and light hot meals. ❸ Dorsoduro 671, Campo San Vio ❶ 041 528 0424 ❶ 08.00–21.00 Mon–Sat ❻ Water bus to Accademia

San Basilio ££ ❾ Traditional Venetian cuisine with a great view of Giudecca island. Also good for a pre-dinner drink. ❸ Dorsoduro 1516, Fondamenta Zattere ❶ 041 521 0028 ❶ 09.30–22.30 Tues–Sat ❻ Water bus to San Basilio

AFTER DARK

The squares of Santa Margherita and San Barnaba and the streets around them are among the few lively parts of Venice after midnight. The quieter Zattere makes for a relaxing post-dinner stroll.

RESTAURANTS

Antico Capon £ ❿ A lively pizzeria with outside tables and pizzas cooked in a wood oven. ❸ Dorsoduro 3004B, Campo Santa Margherita ❶ 041 528 5292 ❶ 12.00–22.30 Tues–Sat ❻ Water bus to Ca' Rezzonico

Trattoria Da Silvio £ ⓫ Modern restaurant with a pretty garden offering pizza and pasta at good prices. ❸ Dorsoduro 3748-3818, Calle San Pantalon ❶ 041 520 5833 ❶ 12.00–23.00, Mar–Oct; 12.00–23.00 Mon–Sat, Nov–Feb ❻ Water bus to San Tomà

Osteria-Enoteca San Barnaba £–££ ⓬ Intimate eatery serving mainly northern Italian meat dishes. Exceptional wine list. ❸ Dorsoduro, Calle Lunga San Barnaba ❶ 041 521 2754 ❶ 12.00–14.30 & 19.00–22.30 Thur–Tues ❻ Water bus to Ca' Rezzonico

Avogaria ££ Chic restaurant with outside tables serving traditional southern Italian dishes from Puglia. ❸ Dorsoduro 1629, Calle d'Avogaria ❶ 041 296 0491 ❷ 11.30–15.00 & 19.30–23.00 Wed–Mon ❷ Water bus to Ca' Rezzonico

Linea d'Ombra ££ Modern décor indoors, but try to get a table on the terrace for fabulous views of Giudecca and San Giorgio. Also pleasant for a pre-lunch or late afternoon drink. ❸ Dorsoduro 19, Ponte dell'Umilta ❷ 09.00–23.00 Thur–Tues ❷ Water bus to Zattere or Salute

Al Gondolieri £££ One of Venice's most elegant restaurants, with rich, tempting food and good wine to match. Pricey but worth it. ❸ Dorsoduro 336, Ponte del Formager ❶ 041 528 6396 ❷ 12.00–15.00 & 19.00–22.00 Wed–Mon ❷ Water bus to Salute

BARS

Café Blue Rock and blues, occasionally played live, in this student bar. ❸ Dorsoduro 3778, Calle de la Scuola ❶ 041 710 227 ❷ 20.00–02.00 Mon–Fri, 17.00–02.00 Sat & Sun ❷ Water bus to San Tomà

Il Caffè Bustling atmosphere and good wine, with live music some evenings. Popular with students. ❸ Dorsoduro 2963, Campo Santa Margherita ❶ 041 528 7998 ❷ 07.00–01.30 Mon–Sat ❷ Water bus to Ca' Rezzonico

Round Midnight Small bar and disco, one of the few places in Venice for dancing. ❸ Dorsoduro 3102, Fondamenta dei Pugni ❶ 041 523 2056 ❷ 21.00–02.00 Thur–Sat, closed July & Aug ❷ Water bus to Ca' Rezzonico

🔺 The Ca' Rezzonico explores 18th-century Venice

San Polo & Santa Croce

The adjoining districts of San Polo and Santa Croce, bordered by
the northern curve of the Grand Canal, form a lively area which is
always buzzing with students. It is fun to get lost wandering around
the maze of tiny streets and canals but if you are in a hurry to get to
one of the important sights in the area it's best to take water bus
no. 1 to the nearest stop.

To relax with a coffee, sit in the lively Campo San Polo, the second
biggest square in Venice and at one time a centre for riotous carnival

THE RIALTO MARKET

For an historic shopping experience buy your souvenirs at the
markets around the Rialto Bridge. The current structure was
designed by Antonio del Ponte, whose surname incidentally
means 'bridge', and completed in 1591. The Rialto is naturally
one of the highest areas in Venice and was the site of one of
the first settlements in the area, allegedly populated as early
as the 5th century. It prospered as the trading centre of the
city from the beginning of the 12th century.

The markets, mostly on the San Polo side of the Grand
Canal, still thrive. There are plenty of stalls selling souvenirs
and trinkets but the real treat is the bustling fish and vegetable
market to the right of the Rialto Bridge. The produce is brought
to the market by barge so get there early with your camera
to catch the unloading and to see the stalls being laid out at
their most colourful and tempting. ● 08.00–12.30 Mon–Sat
(no fish market Mon) ⊗ Water bus to Rialto Mercato

94

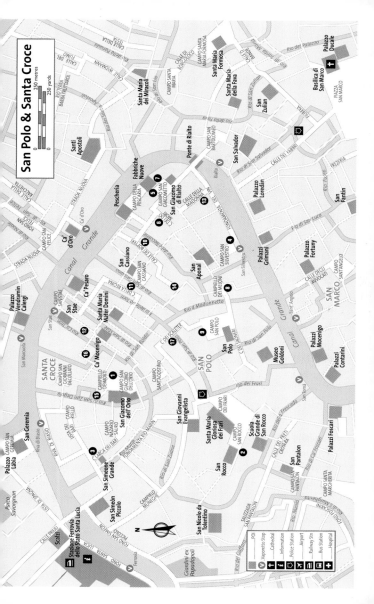

San Polo & Santa Croce

0 — 250 metres
0 — 250 yards

◔ *The famous Rialto Bridge*

festivities. It is surrounded by impressive buildings and has an attractive church, as does the quieter nearby square of San Giacomo dell'Orio. The small, leafy gardens of Giardino Papadopoli, near Piazzale Roma (🕐 08.30–20.00, summer; 08.30–17.30, winter), offer a haven of calm on a hot or busy day.

SIGHTS & ATTRACTIONS

San Polo

Originally built in the Byzantine style in the 9th century, this small church was extensively altered in both the 15th century (Gothic style) and in the 19th century (neoclassical). The bell tower dates from the 14th century. The interior is notable for a luminous cycle of paintings by Giandomenico Tiepolo (1727–1804) as well as work by his more famous father, Gianbattista. You will also find Tintoretto's *Last Supper* and Veronese's *Marriage of the Virgin*. ❸ San Polo 2102, Campo San Polo ❶ 041 275 0462 Ⓦ www.chorusvenezia.org ❶ 10.00–17.00 Mon–Sat Ⓝ Water bus to San Tomà. Admission charge

Santa Maria Gloriosa dei Frari

Built by the Franciscan friars and commonly known simply as Frari, the stark brick exterior of this huge Gothic church gives no indication as to the splendour of the art inside. The current building, in the shape of a Latin cross, dates from the mid-15th century. The bell tower is the second tallest in Venice after the Campanile in St Mark's Square.

The artworks on display include Titian's stunning *Assumption of the Virgin* (1518) dominating the high altar and his *Madonna di Ca' Pesaro* (1526) in the left-hand aisle. Giovanni Bellini's glowing triptych *Madonna Enthroned with Saints* (1488) is in the sacristy on the far right and you can also admire Donatello's wooden statue of John the Baptist (1438). Look out for the highly decorated choir screen, monuments to Titian and to the 15th-century *doge* Foscari, and the grave of the composer Claudio Monteverdi. ❸ San Polo 3072, Campo dei Frari ❶ 041 275 0462 Ⓦ www.chorusvenezia.org ❶ 09.00–18.00 Mon–Sat, 13.00–18.00 Sun Ⓝ Water bus to San Tomà. Admission charge

CULTURE

Ca' Pesaro (Galleria Internazionale d'Arte Moderna)

This imposing 17th-century baroque *palazzo*, built for the wealthy Pesaro family, was the last project undertaken by Venice's great architect Baldassare Longhena. When Longhena died in 1682 the work was taken over by Antonio Gaspari and the building was finished in 1703. You can get some superb views of the Grand Canal from the upper floors.

● *Stop off at the palatial Ca' Pesaro*

Today it houses two art collections. Most of the building is taken up by a gallery of modern art mostly devoted to 19th- and 20th-century Italian painters but also including works by Miro, Matisse, Kandinsky, Klimt and Chagall. On the upper floors is a collection of oriental art and artefacts featuring Japanese arms and armour, paintings, sculpture, musical instruments, pottery and lacquer work. ❸ Santa Croce 2076, Fondamenta Ca Pesaro ❶ 041 524 0662 Ⓦ www.museiciviciveneziani.it Ⓛ 10.00–18.00 Tues–Sun, Apr–Oct; 10.00–17.00 Tues–Sun, Nov–Mar; last entry one hour before closing Ⓝ Water bus to San Stae. Admission charge

Scuola Grande di San Rocco

The opulence of the ornate stone Renaissance façade on this 16th-century *scuola* indicates the wealth of the charitable brotherhood of San Rocco. Set up to help the sick, the association was named in honour of San Rocco (St Roch), patron saint of victims of the plague. The building's most stirring feature is the interior, covered floor to ceiling by the dark, dramatic and anguished visions of Tintoretto, who painted the church over a period of more than 20 years.

Virtually every one of Tintoretto's 54 paintings of scenes from both the New and the Old Testaments is a masterpiece, but his intensely moving *Crucifixion* (1565) in the Salla dell'Albergo is arguably the most outstanding. You will find more works by Tintoretto illustrating the life of St Roch in the Renaissance church of San Rocco next door. ⓐ San Polo 3052, Campo San Rocco ⓣ 041 523 4864 ⓛ 09.00–17.30, Apr–Oct; 10.00–16.00 Nov–Mar, closed Easter ⓦ Water bus to San Tomà. Admission charge

RETAIL THERAPY

Aliani Excellent delicatessen and grocery shop. ⓐ San Polo 654, Ruga Vecchia San Giovanni ⓣ 041 522 4913 ⓛ 08.00–13.00 & 17.00–19.30 Tues–Sat, 08.00–13.00 Mon ⓦ Water bus to San Silvestro

Emporio il Nido delle Cicogne Stylish children's clothes. ⓐ San Polo 2806, Campo San Tomà ⓣ 041 528 7497 ⓛ 09.30–12.30 & 15.30–19.30 Mon–Sat

Kirikù Fashionable clothes for kids. ⓐ San Polo 1463, Calle della Madonetta ⓣ 041 296 0619 ⓛ 09.30–19.30 Mon–Sat, 11.00–19.00 Sun ⓦ Water bus to San Silvestro

Gilberto Penzo Handmade models of gondolas and other boats. ⓐ San Polo 2681, Calle Saoneri ⓣ 041 719 372 ⓛ 10.00–13.00 & 16.00–19.30 Mon–Sat ⓦ Water bus to San Tomà

Hibiscus Colourful jewellery and accessories. 🅐 San Polo 1060, Ruga Rialto 🕿 041 520 8989 🕓 09.30–19.30 Mon–Sat, 11.00–19.00 Sun 🚊 Water bus to San Silvestro

Polliero Fine stationery and book-binding services. 🅐 San Polo 2995, Campo dei Frari 🕿 041 528 5130 🕓 10.00–13.00 & 16.00–19.30 Mon–Sat, 10.00–13.00 Sun 🚊 Water bus to San Tomà

Tragicomica A dazzling array of masks. 🅐 San Polo 2800, Calle dei Nomboli 🕿 041 721 102 🅦 www.tragicomica.it 🕓 10.00–19.00 🚊 Water bus to San Tomà

Zazu Chic designer women's clothing. 🅐 San Polo 2750, Calle Saoneri 🕿 041 715 426 🕓 10.00–13.00 & 15.00–19.30 🚊 Water bus to San Tomà

TAKING A BREAK

Al Prosecco £ ❶ Wine bar serving good, light meals. 🅐 Santa Croce 1503, Campo San Giacomo dell'Orio 🕿 041 524 0202 🕓 08.00–20.00; open later in summer 🚊 Water bus to San Stae

Al Timon £ ❷ Nautical-themed café with tempting sandwiches, *bruschetta* and pasta dishes. 🅐 Campo San Rocco, San Polo 3057 🕿 041 713 120 🕓 07.00–20.30 🚊 Water bus to San Tomà

Alaska £ ❸ Exciting flavours at this ice cream shop. 🅐 Santa Croce 1159, Calle Larga dei Bari 🕿 041 715 211 🕓 11.00–23.00 Apr–Oct; 12.00–21.00 Nov & Jan–Mar, closed Dec 🚊 Water bus to Riva di Biasio

Altrove £ ❹ Popular café near the Rialto Bridge. Have a drink, salad or sandwich. ⓐ San Polo 1105, Campo San Silvestro ❶ 041 528 9224 ⏰ 08.00–24.00 Mon–Sat ⓦ Water bus to San Silvestro

Bancogiro £ ❺ Outside tables by the Grand Canal for a glass of wine, some fresh fish from the nearby market, or a plate of cheese. ⓐ San Polo 122, Campo San Giacometto ❶ 041 523 2061 ⏰ 10.30–23.30 Tues–Sun ⓦ Water bus to Rialto Mercato

● *Cross over the Rialto Bridge, then wander along to Campo San Polo*

Do Mori £ 6 Excellent snacks from the counter. 3 San Polo 429, Calle dei Do Mori 1 041 522 5401 4 08.00–20.30 Mon–Sat 5 Water bus to Rialto Mercato

Naranzaria £ 7 Restaurant and bar with outside tables by the Grand Canal. The Japanese chef serves sushi and impressive salads. 3 San Polo 130, Erbaria 1 041 724 1035 4 11.00–15.00 & 18.00–00.30 Tues–Sun 6 www.naranzaria.it 5 Water bus to Rialto Mercato

Rizzardini £ 8 One of the best bakeries around selling snacks and pastries. 3 San Polo 1415, Campiello dei Meloni 1 041 522 3835 4 07.00–20.30 Wed–Mon 5 Water bus to San Silvestro

Birraria £–££ 9 Popular bar in an animated square. Go for the pizza or pasta, or just have a drink. 3 San Polo 2168, Campo San Polo 1 041 275 0570 4 11.00–23.30 5 Water bus to San Tomà

AFTER DARK

RESTAURANTS

Al Garanghélo £ 10 Friendly place serving hearty meals in the evening, with drinks and lighter snacks during the day. 3 San Polo 1570, Calle dei Botteri 1 041 721 721 4 08.00–22.00 Mon–Sat 5 Water bus to Rialto Mercato

Nono Risorto £ 11 Good pizzas and traditional Venetian food in this lively place with a courtyard and a young clientele. 3 Santa Croce 2337, Sottoportego de la Siora Bettina 1 041 524 1169 4 12.00–14.30 & 19.00–23.00 Fri–Tues 5 Water bus to San Stae

⬤ *The grand façade of the Scuola Grande di San Rocco*

Osteria Mocenigo £ 🔢 Traditional *osteria* serving Venetian meals and snacks. 🔢 Santa Croce 1919, Salizzada San Stae ☎ 041 523 1703 🕐 11.30–15.00 & 18.45–23.00 Tues–Sun 🚤 Water bus to San Stae

Alla Madonna ££ 🔢 Good-value meals and fast service in this packed restaurant near the Rialto Bridge. 🔢 San Polo 594, Calle della Madonna ☎ 041 522 3824 🕐 12.00–14.30 & 19.00–22.00 Thur–Tues 🚤 Water bus to Rialto Mercato

Antiche Carampane ££ 🔢 Excellent fish and seafood in this atmospheric *trattoria* with an outdoor terrace. Mixed reports about the service. 🔢 San Polo 1911, Calle de la Carampane ☎ 041 524 0165 🕐 12.30–14.30 & 19.30–22.30 Tues–Sat 🌐 www.antichecarampane.com 🚤 Water bus to San Silvestro

🔼 *Park your gondola right outside your restaurant*

Il Refolo ££ ⓯ Good views from the outside tables of this
fashionable but pricey pizzeria. Good selection of other
dishes and wines. ❸ Santa Croce 1459, Campiello del Piovan
❶ 041 524 0016 ❷ 12.00–14.45 & 19.00–23.00 Wed–Sun,
19.00–23.00 Tues, closed Nov–Mar ❽ Water bus to Riva di Biasio

La Zucca ££ ⓰ One of the most popular restaurants in town,
this pretty canal-side eatery offers friendly service and a great
menu. No fish, but both carnivores and vegetarians are well
catered for. ❸ Santa Croce 1762, Ponte del Megio ❶ 041 524 1570
❼ www.lazucca.it ❷ 12.00–14.30 & 19.00–23.00 Mon–Sat
❽ Water bus to San Stae

Da Fiore £££ ⓱ Upmarket restaurant specialising in fish and seafood,
not to be confused with other restaurants using the same name.
Art deco interior and formal service. ❸ San Polo 2202A, Calle del
Scaleter ❶ 041 721 308 ❷ 12.30–14.30 & 19.30–22.30 Tues–Sat
❼ www.dafiore.net/restaurant.htm ❽ Water bus to San Tomà

BARS

Ai Postali Outside tables and snacks in this popular late-opening bar
near the railway station. ❸ Santa Croce 821, Fondamenta Rio Marin
❶ 041 715 156 ❷ 19.30–02.00 Mon–Sat, closed two wks Aug
❽ Water bus to Riva di Biasio

Da Baffo £ A lively, late-opening bar favoured by students and
academics. ❸ San Polo 2346, Campo Sant'Agostino ❶ 041 520 8862
❷ 07.30–02.00 ❽ Water bus to San Tomà

Cannaregio

The district of Cannaregio, once Venice's main manufacturing area, is spacious and pleasant with broad canal sides and a fairly simple layout. Shops, bars and hotels tend to be cheaper and the area is more popular with locals than the city centre. The backstreets here in Cannaregio, where over a third of the city's population live, are where you will find the 'real' people in Venice.

The Strada Nova is a broad, hectic street running along the Grand Canal, leading from the Rialto Bridge to the Ca' d'Oro museum and packed with shops and cafés as well as tourists. Equally bustling is the Lista di Spagna near the railway station, full of touristy cafés and shops. To see a bit more of the 'real' Venice you have to venture away from these streets.

The Fondamenta della Sensa and the parallel Fondamenta della Misericordia both offer peaceful walks. Look out for the plaque marking Tintoretto's former house at No. 3399 Fondamenta dei Mori, near the bridge by the Campo dei Mori. From the quayside of Fondamente Nuove you can get fine views of the lagoon, the cemetery island of San Michele and, beyond it, Murano.

SIGHTS & ATTRACTIONS

Gesuiti (Santa Maria Assunta)

Not to be confused with the Gesuati in Dorsoduro, this 18th-century baroque church is the first of those built by the Jesuits in the city. Both the exterior and interior are strikingly ornate, some say to the point of vulgarity. Titian's *Martyrdom of St Lawrence* (1558) is above the altar on the left. ⓐ Campo dei Gesuiti ⓣ 041 528 6579 ⓛ 10.00–12.00 & 16.00–18.00 ⓦ Water bus to Fondamente Nuove

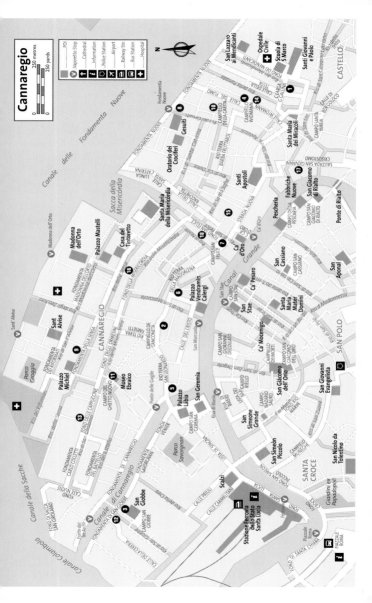

Madonna dell'Orto (Madonna of the Orchard)

This pleasant church in a small square has an attractive red brick façade displaying a marble sculpture of St Christopher, to whom it was originally dedicated. The church was founded in the 14th century and modified in the 15th, making the façade a mixture of Romanesque, Gothic and Renaissance styles. Inside, it is pleasantly peaceful, light and uncluttered. You will find several superb works by Tintoretto, who lived nearby and is buried here in a small chapel off the

● *Inside the lovely Madonna dell'Orto are works by Tintoretto*

right-hand aisle. ⓐ Campo della Madonna dell'Orto ① 041 275 0642
Ⓦ www.chorusvenezia.org ① 10.00–17.00 Mon–Sat ⓦ Water bus to
Madonna dell'Orto. Admission charge

THE JEWISH GHETTO

One of the most interesting areas is the Ghetto, east of the
station and north of the Strada Nova, in which Jews were at
one time confined. A *geto*, or 'foundry', once occupied the area
and this gave its name to other ghettos round the world.

The ghetto was closed off by gates so that between 1516
and the end of the 18th century Jews were allowed out only
during the day and only then if they wore identifiable clothing.
As their numbers grew, they could only build upwards. Napoleon
removed the gates in 1797 but the Austrians who subsequently
occupied Venice confined the Jews again until the end of their
rule in 1866.

Although few Jews live there now, there are still a number
of Jewish shops and synagogues in the area. You can also see
a monument to Holocaust victims transported from Venice
(on a wall in the main square) and visit the small **Museo Ebraico**
(Jewish Museum ⓐ Cannaregio 2902B, Campo del Ghetto Nuovo
① 041 715 359 Ⓦ www.museoebraico.it ① 10.00–19.00 Sun–Fri,
June–Sept; 10.00–18.00 Sun–Fri, Oct–May ⓦ Water bus to San
Marcuola or Guglie). Guided tours in English of the beautiful
hidden synagogues are available at the museum.

Near the Ghetto is the lively **Rio Terra di San Leonardo**
street market (① 08.00–12.30 Mon–Sat ⓦ Water bus to
San Marcuola or Guglie).

Santa Maria dei Miracoli (St Mary of the Miracles)

Popular for local weddings, this church is arguably one of the most beautiful in Venice for its colourful, luminous marble façade. Go early in the morning or late afternoon when the sun falls on its best features. Exquisitely designed in Renaissance style by Pietro Lombardo, it was built in 1481–9 to house an image of the Virgin by Nicolo di Pietro, which was thought to be responsible for a number of miracles. The image is now on display above the high altar.

The interior contains some fine sculptures and also uses coloured marble. Note the 16th-century barrel-vaulted ceiling with its portraits of saints. ② Cannaregio 6075, Campiello dei Miracoli ① 041 275 0462 ⑩ www.chorusvenezia.org ⓛ 10.00–17.00 Mon–Sat ⓝ Water bus to Ca' d'Oro. Admission charge

CULTURE

Ca' d'Oro (House of Gold)

The façade of the 'House of Gold' is one of the most impressive, and best known, of any *palazzo* on the Grand Canal. The building is arguably the prime example of Byzantine-influenced 15th-century Gothic architecture in the city. Built by the aristocratic merchant Marino Contarini in 1420, its exterior was designed to be the most luxurious in Venice, originally featuring gold leaf. After Contarini's death, the subsequent series of owners altered the building substantially, sometimes disastrously. It was restored to its former splendour by Baron Franchetti and left to the state in 1916.

Franchetti's own collection of art, furniture and tapestries is housed in a museum spread over two floors. The highlight is Andrea Mantegna's celebrated *St Sebastian* (1506). Also look out for Carpaccio's early 16th-century *Annunciation and Death of the Virgin*.

● *The Ca' d'Oro should not be missed*

The entrance is in a small alleyway off the Strada Nova and there are excellent views of the Grand Canal and the Rialto markets from both floors. ❸ Cannaregio 3932, Calle della Ca' d'Oro ❶ 041 523 8790 Ⓦ www.cadoro.org ● 08.15–19.15 Tues–Sat, 08.15–14.00 Mon; last entry 30 mins before closing Ⓥ Water bus to Ca' d'Oro. Admission charge

RETAIL THERAPY

Do Maghi Colourful glass vases and other objects with modern designs.
ⓐ Cannaregio 2328 ⓣ 041 524 4719 ⓛ 09.30–13.00 & 14.30–19.00
Mon–Sat, 10.00–19.00 Sun ⓦ Water bus to Rialto

Gian Paolo Tolotti One of Venice's leading antiques shops.
ⓐ Calle del Forno 42 ⓣ 041 528 5262 ⓛ 09.00–12.00 & 16.00–19.00
Mon–Sat ⓦ Water bus to Ca' d'Oro

Laboratorio Blu Children's bookshop with a good selection of English-language books. ⓐ Cannaregio 1224, Campo del Ghetto Vecchio
ⓣ 041 715 819 ⓛ 09.30–12.30 & 16.00–19.30 Tue–Sat, 16.00–19.30
Mon ⓦ Water bus to San Marcuola

◓ *Strada Nuova is the main shopping street in Venice*

Mori & Bozzi Fashionable shoe shop. ⓐ Cannaregio 2367, Rio Terra Maddalena ⓣ 041 715 261 ⓛ 09.30–12.30 & 15.30–19.30 Mon–Sat, 11.00–19.00 Sun ⓝ Water bus to San Marcuola

Vittorio Costantini Glassblower and designer selling intricate glass animals and birds. ⓐ Cannaregio 5311, Calle del Fumo ⓣ 041 522 2265 ⓦ www.popweb.com/costantini ⓛ 09.15–13.00 & 14.15–18.00 Mon–Fri ⓝ Water bus to Fondamente Nuove

TAKING A BREAK

Da Alberto £ ❶ Good hot and cold food in a comforting environment. ⓐ Cannaregio 5401, Calle Larga Giacinto Gallina ⓣ 041 523 8153 ⓛ 10.30–15.00 & 18.00–22.00 Mon–Sat ⓝ Water bus to Ospedale

Boscolo £ ❷ Drinks, pizzas or sweet treats from this bakery. ⓐ Cannaregio 1818, Campiello de l'Anconeta ⓣ 041 720 731 ⓛ 06.40–20.40 Tues–Sun; closed July & Feb ⓝ Water bus to San Marcuola

Canottieri £ ❸ Popular with students for its good-value light lunches or fuller evening meals. Good range of fish. ⓐ Cannaregio 690, Fondamenta di San Giobbe ⓣ 041 717 999 ⓛ 08.00–15.00 & 19.00–23.00 Tues–Sat ⓝ Water bus to Crea or Tre Archi

Cea £ ❹ Good for pasta, salad or simply an outdoor drink. ⓐ Cannaregio 5422A, Campiello Stella ⓣ 041 523 7450 ⓛ 09.00–22.00 Mon–Fri, 09.00–14.30 Sat ⓝ Water bus to Fondamente Nuove

Do Colonne £ ❺ Good range of snacks and sandwiches and a few hot meals. ⓐ Cannaregio 1814C, Rio Terà San Leonardo ☎ 041 524 0453 🕐 10.00–20.30 Sun–Fri Ⓝ Water bus to San Marcuola

Il Gelatone £ ❻ Rich ice cream in an interesting range of flavours. ⓐ Cannaregio 2063, Rio Terra della Maddalena ☎ 041 720 631 🕐 10.30–23.00 May–Sept; 10.30–20.30 Nov–Apr, closed Dec & Jan Ⓝ Water bus to San Marcuola

La Cantina £ ❼ Buzzing, popular bar with excellent snacks. ⓐ Cannaregio 3689, Campo San Felice ☎ 041 522 8258 🕐 11.00–22.00, Tues–Sat Ⓝ Water bus to Ca' d'Oro

Algiubagiò £–££ ❽ Inspiring views of the lagoon from the terrace. ⓐ Cannaregio 5039, Fondamente Nuove ☎ 041 523 6084 🕐 06.30–24.00 Wed–Mon Ⓝ Water bus to Fondamente Nuove

Anice Stellato £–££ ❾ A local favourite, with Venetian specialities made from fresh ingredients, and drinks and snacks outside dining hours. ⓐ Cannaregio 3272, Fondamenta della Sensa ☎ 041 720 744 🕐 10.00–15.00 & 18.30–23.00 Tues–Sun Ⓝ Water bus to Ca' d'Oro

AFTER DARK

RESTAURANTS
Alla Frasca £ ❿ Pretty *osteria* with southern Italian food and good homemade pasta. ⓐ Cannaregio 5176, Campiello della Carita ☎ 041 528 5433 🕐 11.00–15.00 & 18.30–23.00 Wed–Mon Ⓝ Water bus to Fondamente Nuove

Ai Quattro Rusteghi £ ⓫ Friendly staff and outdoor seating make this a pleasurable place to spend an evening. ⓐ Cannaregio 2888, Campo del Ghetto Nuovo ⓣ 041 715 160 ⓦ www.aiquattrorusteghi.com ⓛ 12.00–14.30 & 19.00–23.00 ⓝ Water bus to San Marcuola or Guglie

Dalla Marisa £–££ ⓬ Rich meat and game dishes in this tiny restaurant with canal-side tables. Booking recommended. ⓐ Cannaregio 625B, Fondamenta di San Giobbe ⓣ 041 720 211 ⓛ 12.00–14.30 & 20.00–21.15 Tue & Fri–Sun, 12.00–14.30 Mon, Wed & Thur ⓝ Water bus to Crea

Bea Vita ££ ⓭ Traditional Venetian food with a modern twist. ⓐ Cannaregio 3082, Fondamenta delle Cappuccine ⓣ 041 275 9347 ⓛ 09.00–23.00 ⓝ Water bus to to Sant'Alvise

Boccadoro ££ ⓮ Worth seeking out for its great fresh fish and seafood. Outside tables. ⓐ Cannaregio 5405A, Campiello Widmann ⓣ 041 521 1021 ⓛ 12.30–14.30 & 20.00–23.00 Tues–Sat ⓝ Water bus to Rialto

Ca' d'Oro (Alla Vedova) ££ ⓯ A long-standing favourite with locals, good for a snack during the day or a traditional Venetian meal in the evening. ⓐ Cannaregio 3912, Ramo Ca' d'Oro ⓣ 041 528 5524 ⓛ 11.30–14.30 & 18.30–23.30 Fri, Sat & Mon–Wed, 18.30–23.30 Sun ⓝ Water bus to Ca' d'Oro

Da Rioba ££ ⓰ Bare bricks and beams create a cosy atmosphere, with outdoor seating in summer. Serves Venetian seafood dishes with a twist. ⓐ Cannaregio 2553, Fondamenta della Misericordia ⓣ 041 524 4379 ⓛ 12.00–14.30 & 19.30–22.30 Tues–Sun; closed three wks Jan ⓝ Water bus to Tre Archi or Ca' d'Oro

Fiaschetteria Toscana ££ ⓱ Fine Venetian-style food in a pleasant atmosphere. Excellent desserts. ⓐ Cannaregio 5719, Salizada San Giovanni Crisostomo ⓣ 041 528 5281 ⓛ 12.30–14.30 & 19.30–22.30 Thur–Mon, 19.30–22.30 Wed ⓦ www.fiaschetteriatoscana.it ⓝ Water bus to Rialto

◬ *A beautiful, traditional canal house*

Vini da Gigio ££ ⑱ Good food and extensive wine list in this
romantic but busy restaurant. ➋ Cannaregio 3628A, Fondamenta
San Felice ➊ 041 528 5140 ➌ 12.00–14.30 & 19.30–22.30 Wed–Sun
Ⓦ www.vinidagigio.com Ⓝ Water bus to Ca' d'Oro

BARS

Al Parlamento Bar with disco music some evenings attracting
a young crowd. Sandwiches and snacks available. ➋ Cannaregio 511,
Fondamenta San Giobbe ➊ 041 244 0214 ➌ 08.00–02.00
Ⓝ Water bus to Crea

Fiddler's Elbow A popular Irish pub near Strada Nuova.
➋ Cannaregio 3847, Corte dei Pali gia Testori ➊ 041 523 9930
➌ 17.00–01.00 Ⓝ Water bus to Ca' d'Oro

Iguana Tex-Mex food and music. ➋ Cannaregio 2515, Fondamenta
della Misericordia ➊ 041 713 561 ➌ 18.00–01.00 Tues–Sun
Ⓝ Water bus to Ca' d'Oro

Santo Bevitore Friendly pub with reasonably priced snacks and
live jazz on Mondays. ➋ Cannaregio 2393A, Fondamenta Diedo,
Campo Santa Fosca ➊ 041 717 560 ➌ 07.00–24.00 Mon–Fri,
09.30–01.30 Sat Ⓝ Water bus to San Marcuola

Paradiso Perduto Well-known restaurant, open late with music
in the evenings. ➋ Cannaregio 2540, Fondamenta della Misericordia
➊ 041 720 581 ➌ 12.00–02.00 Thur–Sun, 19.00–02.00 Mon
Ⓝ Water bus to San Marcuola

CASINO CHIC

Venice's smart casino is housed in an early 16th-century Renaissance building on the Grand Canal. A plaque outside commemorates the death of Wagner in the building in 1883. Photo ID and smart dress, including jacket and tie for men, are required. ❸ Palazzo Vendramin Calergi, Cannaregio 2040, Calle Larga Vendramin (off Rio Terra dell Maddalena) ❶ 041 529 7111 Ⓦ www.casinovenezia.it ⏱ 15.30–02.30 Mon–Thur, 15.30–03.00 Fri & Sat Ⓝ Water bus to San Marcuola. Admission charge

THEATRE

Teatro Fondamente Nuove Theatre mainly hosting performances of contemporary dance. ❸ Cannaregio 5013, Fondamente Nuove ❶ 041 522 4498 Ⓦ www.teatrofondamentanuove.it Ⓝ Water bus to Fondamente Nuove

Teatro Malibran Originally built in 1678; performances of opera, ballet and classical music. ❸ Cannaregio 5873, Campiello Malibran ❶ 041 786 601 Ⓦ www.lafenice.it Ⓝ Water bus to Rialto

---

● *The Excelsior Hotel on the Lido*

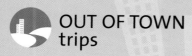

The Lido, Giudecca & San Giorgio Maggiore

The islands of the southern lagoon are just a short trip from the city centre by water bus and are well worth a day trip for their change of atmosphere. There are superb views of Venice from both Giudecca and San Giorgio.

GETTING THERE

You can take water bus nos. 1, 82, 51 or 52 straight to the Lido. No. 1 leaves from all stops along the Grand Canal, and nos. 51 and 52 depart from the San Zaccaria stop, just along from the Palazzo Ducale. It takes no more than 15 minutes from San Zaccaria.

To reach San Giorgio and Giudecca, take water bus no. 82 from anywhere along the Grand Canal or from the San Zaccaria or Zattere stops.

SIGHTS & ATTRACTIONS

THE LIDO

The Lido is Venice's beach resort, a fashionable holiday destination since the early 20th century when the luxurious Excelsior and Des Bains hotels first opened. It is basically a 12 km (8 mile) sandbank with long, straight roads and broad, shaded avenues. Cars are allowed and the area is also a residential suburb. In contrast to Venice, the houses and villas of the Lido are modern in design and many are decorated in art nouveau or art deco styles. The Lido is the place to get away from frantic sightseeing – take the time to relax and enjoy the atmosphere.

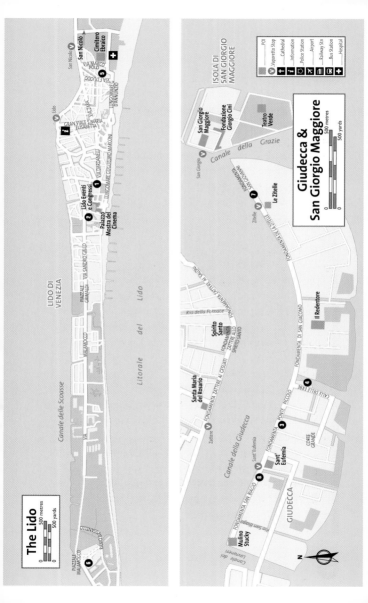

The Lido

0   500 metres
0   500 yards

LIDO DI VENEZIA

Litorale   del   Lido

Canale delle Scoasse

San Nicolò
San Nicolò
VIA NICOLO
Cimitero Ebraico
VIA FILOVIA
VIA MARCO POLO
LUNGOMARE D'ANNUNZIO
GRAN VIALE S MARIA ELISABETTA
VIA LEPANTO
VIA SANDRO GALLO
Lido
LUNGOMARE GUGLIELMO MARCONI
Lido Eventi e Congressi
Palazzo Mostra del Cinema
PIAZZALE GRIMALDI
MALAMOCCO
VIA
PIAZZALE MALAMOCCO
BACIN
OTTINELLO

Giudecca & San Giorgio Maggiore

0   500 metres
0   500 yards

ISOLA DI SAN GIORGIO MAGGIORE

San Giorgio Maggiore
Fondazione Giorgio Cini
Teatro Verde
San Giorgio
Canale   della   Grazie
Le Zitelle
Zitelle
FONDAMENTA DE LA ZITELLE
FONDAMENTA SAN GIACOMO
FONDAMENTA SAN GIACOMO
Il Redentore
Ria della Fornace
Rio de S. Eufemia
FONDAMENTA ZATTERE AL SALONI
Spirito Santo
FONDAMENTA ZATTERE ALLO SPIRITO SANTO
Santa Maria del Rosario
FONDAMENTA ZATTERE AI GESUATI
Zattere
CALLE DELLE ERBE
FONDAMENTA PONTE PICCOLO
Sant'Eufemia
CORTE GRANDE
Sant'Eufemia
GIUDECCA
Canale della Giudecca
FONDAMENTA SAN BIAGIO
Rio San Biagio
Mulino Stucky
Canale del Lavoneri

LEGEND
POI
Vaporetto Stop
Cathedral
Information
Police Station
Airport
Railway Stn
Bus Station
Hospital

N

Beach

The sandbank stretches along most of the southern side of the island, with occasional private areas reserved for hotel guests. In most areas there are huts and umbrellas for hire, but these areas charge an entrance fee. The Blue Moon beach at the end of the Gran Viale is free and the Alberoni and San Nicolò beaches are usually the quietest. The beach is a 15-minute walk from the Gran Viale Santa Maria Elisabetta water bus stop, which is also the departure point for taxis and various regular road bus routes to all parts of the Lido.

VENICE FILM FESTIVAL

The Lido heaves in late August and early September with cinema-lovers flocking for the annual Film Festival. The event is attended by top international film producers and actors hoping for the *Leone D'Oro* (Golden Lion) award and is a showcase for both mainstream and art house films. The area around the multi-screen Palazzo del Cinema and the old Casino buzzes with activity and film stars can be spotted hanging out at the luxurious Excelsior Hotel. The festival actually started at the Excelsior in 1932 – the first cinema event of its kind in the world – and was so successful that the Palazzo del Cinema was built four years later to host it.

You can get season tickets or tickets for individual films, but do book well in advance.

Mostra Internazionale D'Arte Cinematografica

📍 Palazzo del Cinema, Lungomare Marconi 90

📞 041 521 8711 🌐 www.labiennale.org

Malamocco

The village of Malamocco at the western end of the island is a good place to enjoy a lazy meal of excellent fish and seafood. Ⓝ Bus: B

San Nicolò

At the eastern end of the Lido is the San Nicolò area, which has a 15th-century fortress as well as the 11th-century church which forms the main focus of the festival of La Sensa (see page 9). There is also the **Cimitero Ebraico**, a Jewish cemetery dating from 1386 (ⓐ Via Cipro ⓣ 041 715 359 ⓕ 041 72 3007 ⓔ prenotazioni@codesscultura.it), but you must book in advance to visit. Ⓝ Bus: A

Sport

Opportunities for sport and exercise are much better on the Lido than in Venice itself. You can hire a bicycle from **Lido On Bike** (ⓐ Gran Viale 21B ⓣ 041 526 8019 ⓦ www.lidoonbike.it) or **Giorgio Barberi** (ⓐ Gran Viale 79A ⓣ 041 526 14 90), play golf at the **Circolo Golf Venezia** (ⓐ Strada Vecchia 1 ⓣ 041 731 333 ⓦ www.circologolfvenezia.it), enjoy a game of tennis at the **Tennis Club Ca' del Moro** (ⓐ Via Ferruccio Parri 6 ⓣ 041 770 965) or go for a swim at the public swimming pool **Piscina Ca' Bianca** (ⓐ Via Sandro Gallo, Lido ⓣ 041 526 2222).

GIUDECCA

Originally filled with *palazzos* and pleasure gardens, by the 19th century Giudecca had became a site for factories, prisons and warehouses. Reinvented yet again in the 20th century, it is today a pleasant residential suburb of Venice well-known for its luxurious Cipriani hotel (see page 37). Elton John has a property on the island. When you reach Giudecca, look back over Venice from the quayside. The southern end also has some wonderful views of the lagoon.

Giudecca is tiny and it is quick and easy to walk to all destinations. If you do need to use public transport there are three water bus stops: Zitelle, Redentore and Palanca.

Il Redentore

Palladio's magnificent domed church of the Redeemer was built in 1592 to give thanks for the end of a plague which killed 50,000 Venetians. During the colourful Festa del Redentore in late July (see page 10), a pontoon bridge is laid across the Giudecca canal from Zattere to the church.

The façade is in the style of a grand classical temple but the interior is fairly modest, containing paintings by Vivarini and Veronese. ⓐ Giudecca 195, Campo del Redentore ⓣ 041 275 0462 ⓦ www.chorusvenezia.org ⓛ 10.00–17.00 Mon–Sat ⓥ Water bus to Redentore. Admission charge

SAN GIORGIO MAGGIORE

This tiny island, just across the lagoon from St Mark's Square, is worth a visit for its landmark church of the same name and its Benedictine monastery of Fondazione Giorgio Cini.

San Giorgio Maggiore

Andrea Palladio's distinctive style of architecture is clearly visible in the capacious, harmonious and beautifully proportioned interior of this church. Tintoretto's *Last Supper* and *Manna from Heaven* are here as well as works by Carpaccio and Palma il Giovane.

Take the lift up the recently restored bell tower for some wonderful views of Venice and the lagoon. ⓐ Isola di San Giorgio ⓣ 041 522 7827 ⓛ 09.30–12.30 & 14.30–18.30, May–Sept; 09.30–12.30 & 14.30–16.30, Oct–Apr ⓥ Water bus to San Giorgio. Admission charge for bell tower

● *Il Redentore dominates Giudecca's skyline*

⬤ *San Giorgio Maggiore was part of the old Benedictine monastery*

Fondazione Giorgio Cini

This late 10th-century Benedictine monastery once enjoyed considerable wealth and prestige, welcoming powerful visitors such as Florentine Cosimo de' Medici, who commissioned a great library for it in the 15th century.

The monastery was enlarged in the 16th century with a fine refectory and cloisters designed by Andrea Palladio. Its fortunes changed, however, when Napoleon took over and the building became an artillery headquarters.

It was not until 1951 that it was bought by Count Vittorio Cini, carefully restored and turned into an international cultural centre.

It has since hosted major international conferences including the G7 summits of 1980 and 1987. Temporary art exhibitions and concerts complement the permanent collection of works by Tintoretto. Visit is by guided tour only, with regular English-language tours lasting approximately one hour. Check the website for details. ⓐ Isola di San Giorgio ① 041 528 9900 ⓦ www.cini.it ⓒ Guided tours every 30 mins between 10.00–17.00 Sat & Sun ⓝ Water bus to San Giorgio. Admission charge

RETAIL THERAPY

There are several Italian chain stores on the Lido along the Gran Viale, but in general it is best to take a break from shopping when visiting the islands. For a modestly priced department store with a supermarket, head for **Oviesse** ⓐ Via Corfu 1, Lido ① 041 526 5720 ⓒ 09.00–20.00 Mon–Sat, 09.00–16.00 Sun ⓝ Water bus to Lido

TAKING A BREAK & AFTER DARK

Pasticceria Maggion £ ❶ Excellent pastries. ⓐ Via Dardenelli 46A, Lido ① 041 526 0836 ⓝ Water bus to Lido

Trento £ ❷ This popular bar serves simple but tasty food. ⓐ Via Sandro Gallo 82E, Lido ① 041 526 5960 ⓒ 07.00–21.00 Mon–Sat ⓝ Water bus to Lido

Alla Palanca £–££ ❸ A friendly welcome, reasonable prices and a great view. ⓐ Giudecca 448, Fondamenta del Ponte Piccolo ① 041 528 7719 ⓒ 07.00–20.30 Mon–Sat ⓝ Water bus to Palanca

Altanella ££ ❹ Fish restaurant with a pleasant terrace.
ⓐ Giudecca 268, Calle delle Erbe ⓣ 041 522 77 80 ⓛ 12.30–14.00
& 19.30–21.00 Wed–Sun ⓦ Water bus to Palanca

La Favorita ££ ❺ Traditional Venetian dishes in a calm atmosphere.
ⓐ Via Francesca Duodo 33 ⓣ 041 526 1626 ⓛ 12.30–14.30 & 19.30–22.30
Wed–Sun, 19.30–22.30 Tues ⓦ Water bus to Lido

Trattoria Scarso ££ ❻ A simple, traditional fish restaurant in
the village of Malamocco on the Lido. ⓐ Piazzale Malamocco 5
ⓣ 041 770 834 ⓛ 11.00–15.00 & 19.00–23.00 Wed–Mon, Mar–Oct;
11.00–15.00 Wed–Mon, Nov–Feb ⓦ Water bus to Lido

Cip's Club ££–£££ ❼ One of several restaurants at the Cipriani
hotel, with superb views of Venice from the terrace. ⓐ Giudecca 10,
Fondamenta de la Zitelle ⓣ 041 520 7744 ⓛ 19.30–23.30 Apr–Dec;
closed Jan–Mar ⓦ www.cipriani.com ⓦ Water bus to Zitelle

● Enjoy a meal with a view at Cip's

Harry's Dolci ££–£££ ❽ An offshoot of the renowned Harry's Bar, with great views from the terrace. ⓐ Giudecca 773, Fondamenta San Biagio ❶ 041 522 4844 ❷ 10.30–23.00 (drinks and snacks); 12.00–15.00 & 19.00–22.30 (full meals) Wed–Sun, closed Nov–Mar ⓦ www.cipriani.com ⓝ Water bus to Palanca

ACCOMMODATION

Ostello Venezia £ This cheap and cheerful hostel provides clean dorms and family rooms, some of them with private bathrooms. Its location means it is a peaceful haven, whilst offering great views of the city. St Mark's is just a five-minute boat ride away. ⓐ Fondamenta delle Zitelle 86 ❶ 041 523 8211 ⓦ www.ostellionline.org ⓝ Water bus to Zitelle

Belvedere ££ Straightforward hotel near the main water bus stop. ⓐ Piazzale Santa Maria Elisabetta 4, Lido ❶ 041 526 0115 ⓦ www.belvedere-venezia.com ⓝ Water bus to Lido

Villa Cipro ££ Pleasantly decorated rooms and a pretty courtyard. ⓐ Via Zara 2, Lido ❶ 041 731 538 ⓦ www.hotelvillacipro.com ⓝ Water bus to Lido

Hotel des Bains ££–£££ Rooms with a sea or garden view as well as a pool and private beach. ⓐ Lungomare Marconi 17, Lido ❶ 041 526 5921 ⓦ www.starwood.com ❷ Closed Nov–Apr ⓝ Water bus to Lido

Excelsior £££ This luxurious Moorish *palazzo* boasts all creature comforts plus a pool and private beach. ⓐ Lungomare Marconi 41, Lido ❶ 041 526 0201 ⓦ www.starwood.com ❷ Closed Nov–Apr ⓝ Water bus to Lido; regular boat shuttle to Venice for hotel guests

Murano, Torcello & Burano

The ancient lagoon islands of Murano, Torcello and Burano are worth visiting not only to escape from the bustle of Venice but also for the enjoyable trip across the lagoon.

GETTING THERE

Water buses nos. 41 and 42 from Fondamente Nuove will take you straight to nearby Murano. For Torcello and Burano take the Linea LN (Laguna Nord) water bus from either San Zaccaria or Fondamente Nuove.

SIGHTS & ATTRACTIONS

MURANO
Museo del Vetro

Exhibits ranging from ancient Roman glass to modern Murano designs are arranged chronologically in this 17th-century *palazzo*, once home to the bishops of Torcello. It is a great place to get a perspective on the rich history of glass-making behind the island's thriving industry. ⓐ Fondamenta Giustinian 8 ⓣ 041 739 586 ⓦ www.museiciviciveneziani.it ⓛ 10.00–18.00 Thur–Tues, Apr–Oct, 10.00–17.00 Thur–Tues, Nov–Mar; last entry 30 mins before closing ⓝ Water bus to Museo

Santi Maria e Donato

This serene basilica is thought to have been founded as early as the 7th century. The main façade is clearly Byzantine influenced with a colonnaded apse, while the interior has five Greek marble columns

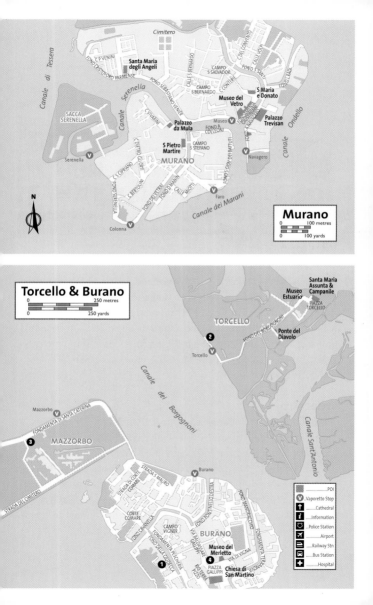

Murano

Cimitero

Canale di Tessera

C P VENINI

FOND CRISTOFORO PARMENSE

Santa Maria
degli Angeli

FOND SEBASTIANO VENIER

Canale Serenella

SACCA
SERENELLA

Canale Serenella

COVARINI

CALLE D BERNARDO
CAMPO
S SALVADOR

CAMPO
S BERNARDO

CONTERIE

CALLE VOLTO

DEL CONVENTO

FOND S CHIARA

FOND D NAVAGERO

CALLE D BRIATI

S Maria
e Donato

Museo del
Vetro

Palazzo
Trevisan

FOND M GIUSTINIAN

Palazzo
da Mula

Museo V

FOND D
COLLEONI

Canale Ondello

Serenella V

C RIVA LONGA

S CIPRIANO

C BERTOLINI

FOND SERENELLA

C RIETRO D'GIOTTI

S Pietro
Martire

CAMPO
S STEFANO

MURANO

FOND DE VETRAI

FOND D MANIN

CALLE D MOTTI

Navagero V

Canale Ondello

Colonna V

Faro V

FOND D DEI BATTUTI

Canale dei Marani

N

0   100 metres
0   100 yards

Torcello & Burano

0   250 metres
0   250 yards

Canale Sant'Antonio

Santa Maria
Assunta &
Campanile

Museo
Estuario

PIAZZA
TORCELLO

TORCELLO

Ponte del
Diavolo

FOND DEL BORGOGNONI

❷

Torcello V

Canale dei Borgognoni

Mazzorbo V

FONDAMENTA DI SANTA CATERINA

MAZZORBO

❸

STRADA DEL CIMITERO

STRADA DI CORTE COMARE

STRADA S MAURO

Burano V

FOND PONTINELLO D'ESTRA

FOND MANTICHIOCHIO

FONDAMENTA TERRANOVA

CORTE
COMARE

CAMPO
VIGNER

FOND CAVANELLA

FONDAMENTA DELLA PESCHERIA

FOND DELLA GIUDECCA

VIA B GALUPPI

PIAZZA
GALUPPI

Museo del
Merletto

CALLE DI VIGNA

VIA D VIGNA

BURANO

❶

❹

Chiesa di
San Martino

■	POI
V	Vaporetto Stop
✝	Cathedral
ℹ	Information
⊙	Police Station
✈	Airport
🚆	Railway Stn
🚌	Bus Station
✚	Hospital

● *Visit Murano for its fascinating glass museum*

down each side. The 12th-century floor and the apse both feature mosaics and the square bell tower is also characteristic of the 12th- and 13th-century Veneto-Byzantine style. The church was restored in the 19th century and retains its original beauty despite missing the top of its steeple. ❸ Campo San Donato ❶ 041 739 056 ● 09.00–12.00 & 15.30–19.00 Mon–Sat, 15.30–19.00 Sun ◐ Water bus to Museo

TORCELLO

Venetians started flocking to Torcello in the 5th and 6th centuries to escape invading tribes. The island had a population of 20,000 by the 14th century and was filled with fine *palazzos* and churches. The marshy land made the area unhealthy, however, and by the 15th century many of its inhabitants escaped the danger of malaria by moving to Venice, which was prospering at the time. Today only a handful of people live here but it is a refreshing contrast to Venice, with a few restaurants and the odd souvenir stall.

Campanile (Bell Tower)

A climb to the top of the basilica's bell tower will give you magnificent views of the lagoon. ⓐ Santa Maria Assunta ⏱ 10.30–17.30, Mar–Oct (last entry 17.00); 10.30–17.00 Nov–Feb (last entry 16.00) Ⓝ Water bus to Torcello. Admission charge

Santa Maria Assunta

The oldest building in the lagoon, this Veneto-Byzantine style basilica dates from as early as 639. Most of what you see today, however, was built in the early 11th century. Look closely at the intricate mosaics on both the floor and walls, in particular the *Madonna and Child* in the central apse, and at the marble choir screen ⓐ Torcello ☎ 041 270 2464 ⏱ 10.30–18.00 Mar–Oct; 10.00–17.00 Nov–Feb; last entry 30 mins before closing Ⓝ Water bus to Torcello. Admission charge

ISLAND TOURS

Another good way of seeing the islands is to take an organised tour. **Alilaguna** (☎ 041 241 1711 🌐 alilaguna.com) runs good value multilingual group tours of the islands, leaving twice a day in summer and once daily in winter, with tours lasting around four hours. For a private tour in English or another language, contact the **Cooperativa Guide Turistiche** (ⓐ San Marco 750, Calle Morosini de la Regina ☎ 041 520 9038 🌐 www.guidevenezia.it ⏱ 09.00–13.00 & 14.00–18.00 Mon–Fri, 09.00–13.00 Sat, June–Aug; 09.00–17.00 Mon–Fri, 09.00–13.00 Sat, Sept–May Ⓝ Water bus to San Zaccaria). Advance booking is advisable.

◆ *Burano has a rather different style to Venice*

BURANO

The vividly coloured houses on the island of Burano make it one of the most picturesque places in the lagoon. It is famous for its lace-making and also has a thriving fishing industry. With a population of just 5,000, it is a quiet and pleasant place to stroll around admiring the intricate lace on sale and seeing the fishermen land their catch, repair their nets or paint their boats.

When you are tired of wandering around, stop for a drink near the church of San Martino with its tilting bell tower or choose a restaurant to enjoy some excellent fresh fish.

RETAIL THERAPY

The only things worth buying – but they really are worth buying – are glass and lace on the islands that make them. Make sure you are buying a genuine product.

MURANO

Barovier & Toso Well-established glass-maker producing impressive contemporary designs. 🄰 Fondamenta Vetrai 28 🕿 041 739 049 🕐 10.00–12.30 & 13.00–17.00 Mon–Fri Ⓥ Water bus to Colonna

MURANO GLASS

Glass-makers began moving from Venice to Murano in the late 13th century. The industry made the island – which is actually nine small islands linked by bridges – prosperous and it once had a population of 30,000. Although only 5,000 people live there today, the industry continues to thrive and Murano glass is exported around the world.

For a unique experience, visit the glass-blowing factories and workshops, many of which will demonstrate their craft for you. There will be plenty of locals on the quayside when you arrive offering to take you to the workshops. By all means go along, but don't feel obliged to tip them or to part with your money before taking a good look round.

Whatever you buy, do check that it is authentic Murano glass and not an inferior, imported product. Look for the Vetro Artistico trademark and be prepared to pay a high price in return for quality. The Retail Therapy section below lists several established quality glass shops.

🔺 *Murano glass is sold all around the world*

Luigi Camozzo Specialist in fine, engraved glass. ⓐ Fondamenta
Venier 3 ⓣ 041 736 875 ⓛ 11.00–13.30 & 14.30–18.00 Mon–Fri
ⓦ Water bus to Venier

Marina e Susanna Sent Contemporary designer glass jewellery.
ⓐ Fondamenta Serenella 20 ⓣ 041 527 4665 ⓛ 10.00–17.00 Mon–Fri
ⓦ Water bus to Colonna

Rossana e Rossana Traditional Venetian glass with modern variations.
ⓐ Riva Lunga 11 ⓣ 041 527 4076 ⓛ 10.00–18.00 Ⓦ Water bus to Museo

Venini Old and new designs in this well-established glass-making
outlet. ⓐ Fondamenta Vetrai 50 ⓣ 041 273 7211 ⓛ 09.30–17.30
Mon–Sat Ⓦ Water bus to Colonna

BURANO

Emilia Arguably the best lace shop on Burano. ⓐ Piazza Baldassare
Galuppi 205 ⓣ 041 735 299 ⓛ 09.00–18.30 Ⓦ Water bus to Burano

Martina Wide range of lace items including clothing. ⓐ Via San
Mauro 307 ⓣ 041 735 523 ⓛ 09.30–18.00 Ⓦ Water bus to Burano

BURANO LACE

The intricate craft of lace-making was traditionally undertaken
by the wives of local fishermen since the 15th century. It almost
died out but was happily revived in the 19th century.

To get a perspective on the history and art of lace-making
visit the **Museo del Merletto** (Lace Museum). Set up in 1871 as
a lace-making school, it now displays some superb examples of
Burano's famously delicate and intricate work, from fans and
gloves to tablecloths. Some exhibits date from the 16th century
and you can also occasionally see current lace-makers at work.
ⓐ Piazza Galuppi 187 ⓣ 041 730 034 Ⓦ www.museiciviciveneziani.it
ⓛ 10.00–17.00 Wed–Mon, Apr–Oct; 10.00–18.00 Wed–Mon,
Nov–March; last entry 15 mins before closing Ⓦ Water bus
to Burano. Admission charge

TAKING A BREAK & AFTER DARK

Al Gatto Nero ££ ❶ One of the friendliest places in the lagoon, with excellent fresh fish. ⓐ Fondamenta della Giudecca 88, Burano ❶ 041 730 120 ❷ 12.00–15.00 & 18.00–22.00 Tues–Sun ❸ Water bus to Burano

Al Trono di Attila ££ ❷ Traditional Venetian food served in a pretty garden. Normally open lunchtime only. ⓐ Fondamenta Borgognoni 7A, Torcello ❶ 041 730 094 ❸ Water bus to Museo

Alla Maddalena ££ ❸ This lunchtime restaurant on a little island near Burano serves game in winter and fish during summer. ⓐ Mazzorbo ❶ 041 730 151 ❷ 12.00–15.00 Fri–Wed ❸ Water bus to Mazzorbo

Da Romano ££ ❹ Traditional lagoon fish and seafood dishes. ⓐ Piazza Galuppi 221, Burano ❶ 041 730 030 ❷ 12.00–15.00 & 18.30–20.00 Mon & Wed–Sat, 12.00–15.00 Sun ❸ Water bus to Burano

ACCOMMODATION

Locanda Cipriani ££–£££ Run by a branch of the Cipriani family since the 1930s, this restaurant and small six-room hotel is one of the best-known places in the lagoon. The simple, elegant restaurant spills out onto a charming terrace and garden and is a good place to enjoy an afternoon drink. ⓐ Piazza Santa Fosca 29, Torcello ❶ 041 730 150 ❷ 12.00–15.00 Mon & Wed–Sun, 19.15–21.00 Fri & Sat ❸ www.locandacipriani.com ❸ Water bus to Torcello

---

❶ *All sorts of water transport whizz up and down the waterways of Venice*

PRACTICAL
information

Directory

GETTING THERE

By air

Venice's main airport Marco Polo (see page 48) has regular direct flights from the UK with British Airways (🅦 www.ba.com), Lufthansa (🅦 www.lufthansa.co.uk), bmi baby (🅦 www.bmibaby.com) and easyJet (🅦 www.easyjet.com). Alitalia (🅦 www.alitalia.com) offers flights via Milan. Ryanair (🅦 www.ryanair.com) flies to Treviso (see page 50) airport, around 40 km (25 miles) from Venice.

There are direct flights to Venice from the USA with Delta (🅦 www.delta.com) and US Airways (🅦 www.usairways.com).

An alternative route is to fly to Milan's Malpensa airport (🅦 www.sea-aeroportimilano.it) and transfer to Venice by direct shuttle or train (🅦 www.trenitalia.it).

Many people are aware that air travel emits CO_2, which contributes to climate change. You may be interested in the possibility of lessening the environmental impact of your flight through the charity Climate Care, which offsets your CO_2 by funding environmental projects around the world. Visit 🅦 www.climatecare.org

RAIL TRAVEL IN STYLE

A luxurious alternative to conventional rail travel is the Orient Express, which offers 28 trips from London to Venice between April and November. The journey takes 31 hours in the luxurious Venice Simplon-Orient Express train, with all meals included in the price. ☎ 0845 077 2222 🅦 www.orient-express.com

By car

Venice is linked to the rest of Italy by major motorways. Travelling to Venice by car, however, is not recommended. You cannot drive anywhere in the city beyond Piazzale Roma and parking is both expensive and limited. See page 50 for advice on parking.

By coach

Coach travel is one of the cheapest but slowest ways to reach Venice from the UK. The journey takes 25–30 hours from London Victoria coach station. Contact **Eurolines** ☎ 08705 143 219 Ⓦ www.eurolines.com

By rail

The journey by train from London St Pancras International to Venice takes just over 17 hours, changing in Paris. If you fly to Milan and want to take the train to Venice from there, the journey takes around three hours.

For further information on rail travel within Italy see **Trenitalia** Ⓦ www.trenitalia.it

Rail Europe offers information on train travel in Europe, including reservations and tickets. Ⓦ www.raileurope.co.uk

The monthly *Thomas Cook European Rail Timetable* gives up-to-date schedules for European international and national train services. ☎ 01733 416 477 (UK); 1 800 322 3834 (USA) Ⓦ www.thomascookpublishing.com

ENTRY FORMALITIES

EU citizens can remain in Italy for an unlimited period but should register with the city council after 90 days. Visitors from the US, Canada, Australia and New Zealand do not need visas for stays of up to three months, but South African visitors do require a visa. Everyone must show a valid passport or identity card (EU citizens only) upon entry to Italy.

EU citizens do not have to declare goods imported or exported as long as they are for their personal use and they have arrived from another country within the EU. For non-EU citizens or arrivals from outside the EU, the following import restrictions apply: 400 cigarettes or 200 small cigars or 100 cigars or 500 g of tobacco; 1 litre of spirits or 2 litres of fortified wine; 50 g of perfume; €10,000 in cash. See Ⓦ www.agenziadogane.it for more information on customs regulations.

⬤ *Water buses are reliable and comfortable*

MONEY

Italy is a member of the European Union and the euro (€) is the official currency. There are seven banknotes: €5, €10, €20, €50, €100, €200 and €500. Coins come in denominations of €1, €2 and 1, 2, 5, 10, 20 and 50 cents.

There are 24-hour ATM machines located outside most banks, as well as at airports and railway stations, accepting Cirrus, Maestro, Visa and Mastercard.

Foreign currencies and traveller's cheques can be changed at most banks and bureaux de change with a passport or other ID, or at hotels for a hefty commission.

Visa and Mastercard credit cards are commonly accepted in larger stores and hotels but be aware that many bars, cafés, small shops and restaurants do not accept credit and debit cards. Make sure you have some cash in euros, particularly when you arrive.

HEALTH, SAFETY & CRIME

Tap water is safe to drink in Venice and hygiene standards in restaurants are high. Be careful of eating too much seafood if you are not used to it and take mosquito repellent in summer.

UK citizens are entitled to the same medical care as Italians on production of a European Health Insurance Card (EHIC Ⓦ www.ehic.org.uk). Your hotel or the tourist office should be able to advise you of local surgeries and doctors on call. You will have to pay upfront for your visit so don't forget to keep proof of payment in order to be reimbursed when you arrive home. Medicine and tests may cost extra and dentists are not covered by the EHIC. It is advisable to take out comprehensive travel insurance.

Non-EU nationals are entitled to free emergency medical care but should take out medical insurance for all other situations.

Pharmacies (*farmacie*) have green cross signs outside and staff are qualified to give advice about minor ailments. If you use a particular medication regularly it is a good idea to take a stock with you.

Venice is generally safe for travellers, although as with any city you should avoid walking alone at night and in quiet streets. Pick-pocketing, unfortunately, is common in San Marco, the Rialto and other crowded areas including the railway station and water buses. Make sure you keep your wallet safely hidden, your bags zipped shut, and your cameras firmly in your hand with the strap around your neck. Leave your passport and valuables in the hotel safe.

LOST PROPERTY

The main *ufficio oggetti trovati* (lost property office) is at ⓐ San Marco 4136, Riva del Carbon ⓣ 041 274 8225 ⓛ 08.30–12.30 Mon–Fri, 14.30–16.30 Mon & Thur. If you lose a belonging while using public transport, contact the ACTV office at Santa Croce or Piazzale Roma ⓣ 041 2722 1279 ⓛ 07.00–19.30. The Santa Lucia railway station lost property office is on platform 14 ⓣ 041 785 531

OPENING HOURS

Most major attractions are open between 09.00 or 10.00 and 18.00, closing on Mondays. Winter opening hours are generally shorter, and smaller museums and churches may close for lunch.

Banks generally open 08.30–13.00 Mon–Fri, and sometimes 14.45–15.45. They are closed on public holidays and work shorter hours the day before.

Shops open 09.00 or 10.00 until 19.00 or 19.30 Mon–Sat, sometimes closing for lunch. Some shops close on Mondays. All-day and Sunday opening is common in tourist hotspots. Most

● *The police patrol Venice's waterways*

supermarkets are open 09.00–19.30 Mon–Sat. Food markets are open from early in the morning until midday. The Rialto tourist market is open all day but the food market closes at noon.

Pharmacies are usually open 09.00–13.00 & 16.00–20.00 Mon–Sat. Details of out-of-hours pharmacies are posted on a sign on the door.

The opening hours of bars, cafés and restaurants vary greatly, but very few in Venice are open past midnight. Hot meals are generally only served at specific times – around 12.00–14.30 for lunch and 19.00–22.00 for dinner – but snacks may be served throughout the day.

❶ Many establishments, particularly restaurants, close for two weeks in winter and again in July or August.

TOILETS

Public toilets in Venice are relatively well signposted and are normally open 08.00–20.00. Be prepared to pay a small fee, usually €0.50. There are two public toilets near St Mark's Square (one at the Giardini Reali) and others at the Rialto, the railway station, Piazzale Roma, in front of the Accademia Gallery and in the districts of Cannaregio and Castello.

Museums sometimes have clean toilets in the publicly accessible areas near the entrance. Hotels are also a good bet. If you want to use the toilet in a bar or café it is polite to have a quick drink there also.

CHILDREN

Children are welcome in most restaurants and cafés, particularly the simpler ones, and there are plenty of ice cream and cake shops to keep them fed and happy. Public places, including restaurants and bars, are now smoke-free by law.

Baby food, nappies and other children's essentials are best bought from supermarkets and some pharmacies may also stock what you need. Supermarkets tend to be fairly hard to find in the city centre so try to bring adequate supplies, along with any medication, with you from home. Try the **Coop** (ⓐ Santa Croce 506A, Piazzale Roma ⓛ 08–20.00) or **Punto Sma** (ⓐ Dorsoduro 3017, Campo Santa Margherita ⓛ 08.30–20.00 Mon–Sat).

Your children may not be thrilled at the idea of traipsing round museums and churches but they'll love the views from the top of the Campanile in St Mark's Square (see page 64) and the scale models at the excellent Naval History Museum (see page 72). The Peggy Guggenheim Collection (see page 86) offers children's workshops on Sundays and some civic museums also organise family days (see ⓦ www.museiciviciveneziani.it). The dungeons at the Doge's Palace (see page 65) are always popular.

Sometimes the simplest activities are the best – just crossing the canal on a gondola, taking a ride on the water bus or splashing out on a spin in a water taxi can be a great way to keep them entertained. If you are confident handling a boat yourself, hire a small one from **Cristiano Brussa** (ⓐ Cannaregio 1030, Fondamenta di Cannaregio ⓣ 041 275 0196 ⓦ www.cristianobrussa.com).

Green spaces in Venice aren't huge, but Campo Santo Stefano (see page 69), Campo San Polo (see page 94) and the Giardini Pubblici in Castello (see page 60) are fine for a lazy afternoon playing around. If you visit during the Biennale festival (see page 9), you can spend long, happy afternoons visiting the exhibitions in the Arsenale.

For a change of scenery, take children to watch the glass-blowing demonstrations on the island of Murano (see page 135), or the lace-making on Burano (see page 137). And for most children, you can't go wrong if you buy a bucket and spade and head to the Lido for some beach-side fun (see page 122).

COMMUNICATIONS

Internet

Internet cafés, Wi-Fi and hotels offering internet access are increasingly available in Venice, although internet access in any form is rarely cheap. Photo ID is required at internet cafés.

Casanova Music Café An internet café that turns into a disco late at night. ⓐ Cannaregio 158 A, Lista di Spagna ⓣ 041 275 0199 ⓛ Internet: 09.30–23.00

Internet Corner ⓐ Castello 6661A, Barbaria delle Tole ⓣ 041 277 0515 ⓛ 10.00–22.00 Mon–Sat

Internet Point ⓐ Dorsoduro 3812A, Calle dei Preti ⓣ 041 714 666 ⓛ 09.15–20.00

Phone

Phone boxes take *schede telefoniche* (phone cards), which can be bought at news stands or *tabacchi* (tobacconists). Calling rates from phone boxes and hotels tend to be very high. If you travel to Italy often, it may be worth purchasing an Italian SIM card for your mobile.

Telephoning Venice

The area code for the whole of Venice, including the Lido and lagoon islands, is 041. Telephone numbers beginning 800 are toll-free, and numbers beginning 03 are mobile phones. The international dialling code

TELEPHONING ABROAD
From Italy, dial 00, followed by your country code (UK 44;
Republic of Ireland 353; USA and Canada 1; Australia 61;
New Zealand 64; South Africa 27), followed by the area code
(leaving out the first 'o' if there is one) and then the local
number you require.

for Italy is 39. To call Venice from abroad, dial either 00 (from the UK),
011 (from the US) or 0011 (from Australia), followed by the international
code (39), followed by the area code (041) and then the local number
you require. Note that, unlike in many countries, when telephoning
Italy from abroad you do not drop the initial 'o' of the area code.

Post

Postal services in Italy are as reliable as anywhere in Europe. It is
worth paying a little extra for *poste priorità* (express post), which
needs a special *priorità* sticker, as this will ensure your letters arrive
quickly. Post boxes are red and affixed to building walls. They have
two slots – one for letters to be delivered within Venice (*per la Città*)
and one for all other destinations and abroad (*Altre Destinazioni*).
Stamps can be bought in tobacconists as well as in post offices
(*ufficio postale*).

Central post office ⓐ San Marco 5554, Salizada del Fontego dei
Tedeschi (near the Rialto Bridge) ⓒ 08.30–18.30 Mon–Sat

ELECTRICITY

Electrical current in Italy is 220V AC and plugs are the standard
European two round-pin ones. British appliances will need a simple

adaptor, available in airports and hardware stores but best obtained in the UK before travelling. US and other equipment designed for 110v will usually need a transformer (*transformatore di corrente*).

TRAVELLERS WITH DISABILITIES

Venice is an old city and not naturally suited to travellers with physical disabilities. The canals, steep bridges and narrow bumpy streets can be a challenge, particularly when it is crowded. Access facilities are improving rapidly, however, with ramps over bridges and lifts in museums being installed. Importantly, all ACTV water buses are step-free and fairly easy to negotiate for travellers in wheelchairs. Gondolas require several steps and some agility to board.

Be aware that not all hotels and restaurants advertising disabled access actually have accessible facilities such as disabled toilets. Many hotels and museums do not have lifts. It is best to check beforehand and be clear about your needs. There are public disabled toilets on four bridges in the San Marco district requiring special access keys, which you can borrow from the tourist office.

Private beaches on the Lido have disabled toilets, which you can use if you hire a beach hut or umbrella for the day. There are public disabled toilets on the Lido and on the islands of Torcello, Burano and Murano.

Thankfully, there is a good source of up-to-date information on accessibility available from the Informhandicap service at the city council's Ufficio Relazioni con il Pubblico (public relations office), including specific brochures, guides and maps of the city indicating the location of disabled toilets and bridges with wheelchair ramps. ⓐ Ca' Farsetti, San Marco 4136 ⓣ 041 274 8945 ⓦ www.comune.venezia.it/handicap ⓔ informahandicap@comune.venezia.it ⓛ 09.00–13.00 Mon, Tue & Thur–Sat, 09.00–13.00 & 15.00–17.00 Wed

RADAR is the main source of information for UK-based travellers. ⓐ 12 City Forum, 250 City Rd, London EC1V 8AF ☎ 0207 250 3222 🌐 www.radar.org.uk

SATH (Society for Accessible Travel & Hospitality) advises US-based travellers with disabilities. ⓐ 347 Fifth Ave, Suite 610, New York, NY 10016 ☎ 212 447 7284 🌐 www.sath.org

TOURIST INFORMATION

Venice's local tourist information office is APT (Azienda Promozione Turistica di Venezia). It is an excellent source of information, supplying maps, events listings and guidebooks. It does not offer an accommodation booking service but can provide lists and advice. See also their helpful website 🌐 www.turismovenezia.it. Offices are open all year round except at Christmas and New Year.

USEFUL WEBSITES

Water bus, road bus and ferry services: 🌐 www.actv.it
The city council: 🌐 www.comunevenezia.it
The main churches: 🌐 www.chorusvenezia.org
Civic museums: 🌐 www.museicivicivenezian.it
Maps and events listings: 🌐 www.ombra.net and www.veniceonline.it
Transport and events: 🌐 www.hellovenezia.com
Carnival: 🌐 www.carnivalofvenice.com
The on-line version of the excellent listings magazine *Un Ospite di Venezia* (A Guest in Venice): 🌐 www.aguestinvenice.com. Printed copies are available from tourist offices and hotels.

Lido 🖂 Gran Viale Maria Elisabetta 6A ☎ 041 526 57 21
🕐 09.00–12.30 & 15.30–18.00 June–Oct
Marco Polo airport ☎ 041 541 5887 🕐 09.30–19.30
Piazzale Roma 🖂 ASM Garage (located within the garage)
☎ 041 241 1499 🕐 09.30–13.00 & 13.30–16.30
San Marco 🖂 71 F, Piazza San Marco ☎ 041 529 8711 🕐 09.00–15.30
San Marco 🖂 2, Giardini Reali ☎ 041 529 8711 🕐 10.00–18.00
Santa Lucia railway station ☎ 041 529 8711 🕐 08.00–18.30

BACKGROUND READING

Don't Look Now by Daphne Du Maurier. Du Maurier's short story
was made into a controversial Anglo-Italian thriller movie in the 70s.

Painting in 16th century Venice by David Rosand. The esteemed art historian from Colombia University offers insights into many of the works you will see during your stay.

The Architecture of Venice by Deborah Howard. The definitive guide to the architecture of the city.

The Merchant of Venice by William Shakespeare.

The Wings of the Dove by Henry James. Heartrending 1902 novel about an American heiress.

Venice: A Maritime Republic by Frederick C. Lane. A succinct account of the history of Venice as a major sea power.

⊙ *Venetian windows line the canals*

Emergencies

The following are free-pay emergency numbers:

Ambulance ☎ 118

Coastguard ☎ 1530

Fire ☎ 115

Police ☎ 112

MEDICAL SERVICES

Ospedale Civile is Venice's main hospital with a 24-hour *Pronto Soccorso* (Accident & Emergency) department ⊕ Castello 6777, Campo Santi Giovanni e Paolo ☎ 041 529 4111

Ospedale al Mare is the Lido's hospital ⊕ Lungomare D'Annunzio 1, Lido ☎ 041 529 5234

POLICE

There are three types of police in Venice: the para-military *carabinieri*; the *polizia* (state police), and the *vigili* (local police). All will help in an emergency and there are plenty patrolling tourist areas.

If you are the victim of a crime go straight to a *questura* (police station) to make a report. You may need the paperwork to claim on your insurance. There are police stations at:

⊕ Castello 4693A, Campo San Zaccaria ☎ 041 520 4777

Ⓝ Water bus: San Zaccaria

⊕ Castello 5053, Fondamenta di San Lorenzo ☎ 041 271 5511

Ⓝ Water bus: San Zaccaria

⊕ Santa Croce 500, Piazzale Roma ☎ 041 271 5511 Ⓝ Water bus: Piazzale Roma

⊕ Via Dardenelli 52, Lido ☎ 041 220 7911

EMBASSIES & CONSULATES

Australian Embassy ⓐ Via Antonio Bosio 5, Rome ⓣ 06 852 721
ⓦ www.italy.embassy.gov.au

British Consulate ⓐ Piazza Donatori di Sangue 2, Mestre ⓣ 041 505 5990

British Embassy ⓐ Via XX Settembre 80, Rome ⓣ 06 4220 0001
ⓦ www.britishembassy.gov.uk/italy

Canadian Embassy ⓐ Via G.B. de Rossi 27, Rome ⓣ 06 445 981
ⓦ www.canada.it

Irish Embassy ⓐ Piazza di Campitelli 3, Rome ⓣ 06 697 9121
ⓦ www.abasciata-irlanda.it

New Zealand Embassy ⓐ Via Zara 28, Rome ⓣ 06 441 7171
ⓦ www.nzembassy.com

South African Consulate ⓐ Santa Croce 466G, Piazzale Roma, Venice
ⓣ 041 524 1599 ⓦ www.sudafrica.it

US Embassy ⓐ Via Veneto 119, Rome ⓣ 06 46741 ⓦ www.usembassy.it

USEFUL PHRASES

Help!	**Fire!**	**Stop!**
Aiuto!	Al fuoco!	Ferma!
Ahyootaw!	*Ahl fooawcaw!*	*Fairmah!*

Call an ambulance/a doctor/the police/the fire service!
Chiamate un'ambulanza/un medico/la polizia/i pompieri!
*Kyahmahteh oon ahmboolahntsa/oon mehdeecaw/la
pawleetsya/ee pompee-ehree!*

INDEX

WHAT'S IN YOUR GUIDEBOOK?

Independent authors Impartial up-to-date information from our travel experts who meticulously source local knowledge.

Experience Thomas Cook's 165 years in the travel industry and guidebook publishing enriches every word with expertise you can trust.

Travel know-how Contributions by thousands of staff around the globe, each one living and breathing travel.

Editors Travel-publishing professionals, pulling everything together to craft a perfect blend of words, pictures, maps and design.

You, the traveller We deliver a practical, no-nonsense approach to information, geared to how you really use it.

Editorial/project management: Lisa Plumridge
Copy editor: Monica Guy
Layout/DTP: Alison Rayner
Proofreader: Yvonne Bergman

The publishers would like to thank the following companies and individuals for supplying their copyright photographs in this book: Francesco Allegretto, pages 7, 19, 28, 36, 39, 59, 77, 101 & 119; Bill Casey/BigStockPhoto.com, page 82; Paul Gardner/iStockphoto.com, page 104; Picture Colour Library, page 43; Roland Nagy/SXC.hu, page 13; Margarit Ralev/SXC.hu, page 139; Bruno Schievano/SXC.hu, page 152; Alexander Wallnöfer/SXC.hu, page 14; Anwer Bati, all others.

Send your thoughts to
books@thomascook.com

- **Found a great bar, club, shop or must-see sight that we don't feature?**
- **Like to tip us off about any information that needs a little updating?**
- **Want to tell us what you love about this handy little guidebook and more importantly how we can make it even handier?**

Then here's your chance to tell all! Send us ideas, discoveries and recommendations today and then look out for your valuable input in the next edition of this title.

Email the above address (stating the title) or write to:
CitySpots Project Editor, Thomas Cook Publishing, PO Box 227, Coningsby Road, Peterborough PE3 8SB, UK.